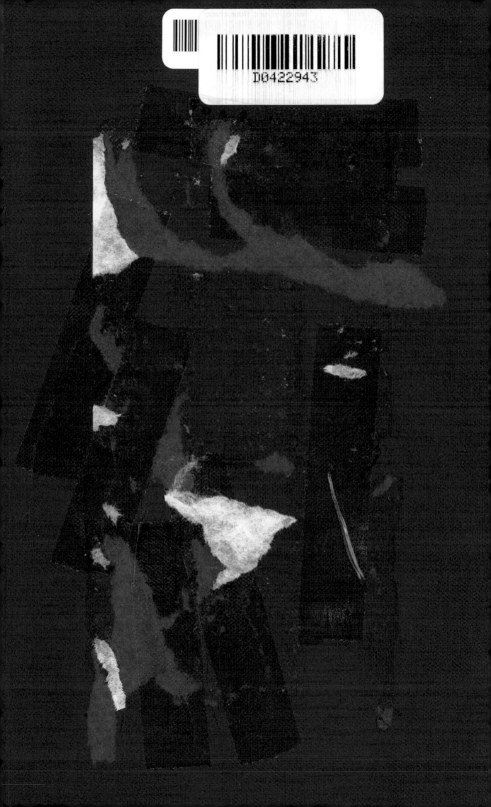

D0422943

Call Me Lucky

Call Me Lucky
A Texan in Hollywood

Robert Hinkle

with Mike Farris

With a foreword by George Stevens, Jr.

UNIVERSITY OF OKLAHOMA PRESS : NORMAN

Library of Congress Cataloging-in-Publication Data

Hinkle, Robert, 1930–
    Call me lucky : a Texan in Hollywood / Robert Hinkle with Mike Farris ; with
a foreword by George Stevens, Jr.
        p. cm.
    ISBN 978-0-8061-4093-3 (hardcover : alk. paper)
        1. Hinkle, Robert, 1930–   2. Motion picture industry—California—Los
Angeles—Biography.   3. Dialogue coaches—California—Los Angeles—
Biography.   4. Stunt performers—California—Los Angeles—Biography.
5. Producers and directors—California—Los Angeles—Biography.
6. Hollywood (Los Angeles, Calif.)—Biography.   7. Los Angeles (Calif.)—
Biography.   8. Texas—Biography.   9. Hinkle, Robert, 1930—Friends and
associates—Anecdotes.   10. Motion picture actors and actresses—California—
Los Angeles—Biography—Anecdotes.   I. Farris, Mike, 1955 June 30–
II. Title.
    PN1998.3.H555A3 2009
    791.45092—dc22
    [B]

                                                                2009014540

1 2 3 4 5 6 7 8 9 10

To my loving wife, Sandy, who has made
this ol' boy the luckiest man alive

Contents

Illustrations

Foreword

I met Bob Hinkle on the set of *Giant* in 1955. Bob was tall and lean and lived under a tan western hat. To those who worked on *Giant,* Bob was known as the "Texas talk" man.

My father, George Stevens, had interviewed Bob for a role in *Giant* and was struck by his natural Texas accent. Dad was a director who insisted on authenticity in his pictures. He called Bob back not to play a role in the film but to work with Rock Hudson and the other actors to give them a sense of how a real Texan talks. Bob helped Rock, Jimmy Dean, Dennis Hopper, Carroll Baker, and Mercedes McCambridge with their accents and taught Jimmy some clever moves with a rope.

Bob was a great spirit on *Giant.* His natural friendliness was a lubricant that helped bring together the large company of actors and crew. One time when the company was shooting in Marfa, Texas, Bob organized a trip to a little town to the north named Kermit. Some local good old boys picked us up in air-conditioned Cadillacs and drove us to the small town. I rode up with Bob and Rock and Jimmy Dean in one car. Elizabeth Taylor and her husband of the day, Michael Wilding, rode in another car. We were expecting dinner at one of the houses where we were staying but learned on arrival that the good old boys had planned a party at the local Rotary Club for several hundred people.

The presence of the three movie stars in this small town created a great deal of excitement—and is probably still talked about in those parts.

Bob Hinkle has led a fascinating life. He was involved in the Berlin Airlift while serving in the U.S. Air Force after World War II. He was also a first-rate rodeo competitor, had a show business career as actor and producer, and enjoyed success as a personal manager and impresario.

We have known one another for over fifty years. We don't meet often, but when we talk on the phone it always ends up being a long reminiscence of the magical time when we worked on *Giant*—a film destined to live as a classic of American cinema.

I am glad Bob Hinkle has decided to tell his own story—which, considering that Bob is a Texan, should contain some tall stories.

George Stevens, Jr.
Washington, D.C.

Preface

When I was ten years old, Tom Mix came to my hometown of Brownfield, Texas. I knew then that I wanted to be a movie cowboy. I never dreamed at the time that it would happen, but life has a funny way of putting you in the right place at the right time. Through luck and the grace of God, I've had a whirlwind career in the picture business that allowed me to bring my own brand of Texas to such notables as James Dean, Rock Hudson, and Elizabeth Taylor in the movie *Giant*; to Paul Newman, Melvyn Douglas, and Patricia Neal in the movie *Hud*; and to Robert Wagner and Natalie Wood in the movie *All the Fine Young Cannibals*.

I helped promote or manage the careers of such stars as Chill Wills, Marty Robbins, and Evel Knievel. I produced short subjects for Paramount and made movies and country music videos for Universal. I filmed rodeos and even took a leak with the president of the United States. I worked with a veritable Hollywood "Who's Who" that also included John Wayne, Joel McCrea, Clint Eastwood, James Arness, Joan Collins, Clark Gable, Marilyn Monroe, Robert Mitchum, Walter Brennan, and Ginger Rogers.

To this day, I still claim as friends many of those with whom I worked or whose paths I crossed—some still living, others not. Those who have gone on include Jimmy Dean,

Paul Newman, Chill Wills, Elvis Presley, Roger Miller, Marty Robbins, and Evel Knievel.

I have tried to stay true to the gist of conversations that occurred as long as fifty or more years ago, though obviously exact quotes, for the most part, escape my memory. From beginning to end, this is not just a story about making movies, but it's a story about an ol' rodeo cowboy who brought west Texas to Hollywood. It's about a man who, to this day, still feels he was damn blessed to do the things he did and meet the folks he met.

When I look back over my life, I can only say, "Call me lucky."

PART I

I'd Rather Be Lucky

CHAPTER ONE

A Texan in Hollywood

Mr. Stevens, to tell you the truth, I've been going to a speech
coach to try to lose this damn accent.

—BOB HINKLE

F or a west Texas cowboy turned two-bit actor, the phone
call from an agent at Famous Artists Agency that early
spring day in 1955 seemed like the stuff of fantasy. "Are you
available to meet with Mr. George Stevens?" she asked.

George Stevens, the producer and director of *Shane* and
A Place in the Sun. Of *Gunga Din,* for crying out loud. A man
who was a legend in Hollywood, whose career started before
I was born. The man who was currently casting for his next
production, a big-screen adaptation of *Giant,* Edna Ferber's
sprawling epic about Texas cattlemen and oil barons. Was I
available to meet with *that* George Stevens?

Hell yes, I was available!

I had been at his office just yesterday for a quick meeting,
sent over by my agent. He had barely acknowledged my presence, not even getting up from his desk to shake my hand.
"I'm not going to start casting the smaller parts for another
month," he said. "Right now I'm concentrating on the leads."

With that, he dismissed me. But now, scarcely a day later,
he was calling me back to his office. So the reason for today's
meeting was obvious: he needed a bona fide Texan to play the
role of Jett Rink opposite Rock Hudson's Bick Benedict and

3

Elizabeth Taylor's Leslie Benedict. After all, *Giant* wasn't just words in a book or a script for me. I had grown up in west Texas with the likes of Bick Benedict and Jett Rink and Uncle Bawley and Bale Clinch. I had worked ranches like the Reata and had eaten west Texas dirt most of my life. I *knew* the characters in *Giant*. Hell, I *was* a character in *Giant*.

Oh sure, Stevens had already cast James Dean in the role of Jett, but in my opinion no way could he breathe life into the character the way I could. Besides, Hollywood was awash in rumors about Dean. *East of Eden* had just been released as a rousing success, and he was now filming *Rebel Without a Cause*. He'd be dropping out of *Giant* any day, and every young actor west of the Rockies and a few east of them was lining up to read for the part. But none of them could match me for pure west Texas. No sirree Bob! That part had Bob Hinkle written all over it. I was about to be discovered. I'd go down in Hollywood history. They'd be talking about me in the same breath as Lana Turner getting discovered in Schwab's Drugstore.

I dressed in my cowboy "uniform": starched jeans with creases in them (what every real cowboy would wear), a freshly starched white shirt, my best boots, and a Stetson 100—the best western hat you could buy at the time. I topped it off with my gold and silver rodeo trophy belt buckle.

It was a beautiful day, clear blue skies with a cool breeze. As I drove from my home in Studio City to Warner Brothers in Burbank, with snow-capped mountain peaks in the distance surrounding the San Fernando Valley, visions of adoring fans and signing autographs danced in my head. I mentally spent the money I was sure to earn, not only from my role in *Giant* but also from all the parts likely to be thrown at my feet after my unforgettable performance. No more "Cowboy A—Bob Hinkle" or "Cowboy Number 3—Bob Hinkle" at the tail end of film credits rolling to empty theaters. Nope, my credits were going to start reading "*Starring* Robert Hinkle." A new Texas legend was about to be born.

George Stevens's office was toward the rear of the Warner Brothers lot, near the trademark water tower. I entered and announced myself. The outer office was furnished western style, with plenty of leather, and sketches of the characters from *Giant* adorned the walls. The day before, his secretary had been cordial enough, but now it seemed as if I had been bumped up to the "be nice to this guy" list.

She buzzed the intercom. "Mr. Stevens, Mr. Hinkle is here."

Now, that had a nice ring to it. "Mr. Hinkle." Up until then I had played only bit parts or done stunt work in westerns, but the winds of change were a-shifting and good fortune was about to blow my direction.

Mr. Stevens hustled out of his office, all smiles and hand-shakes. He was about fifty years of age, a little shy of six feet, and well fed. With his thick hair combed straight back and his open expression, he seemed like a guy a feller would like. He pumped my hand as if we were long-lost buddies who hadn't seen each other in years.

"How you doing, Bob? Great to see you again. Come on in."

As he escorted me into his office, he turned to his secretary. "Get Fred Guiol and Henry Ginsberg over here as soon as possible."

Fred Guiol was the screenwriter for *Giant,* and Henry Ginsberg was Mr. Stevens's producing partner. There was only one possible reason he could want them to meet me: I was about to officially become the next Jett Rink. I wondered if Mr. Stevens could see my heart pounding through my shirt or maybe even hear it. It was sure pounding in my ears—*ka-thump ka-thump.*

He led me into his wood-paneled office, also furnished with lots of leather. I took a seat across from his massive oak desk that was covered with papers. While he rustled through the stacks of paper, looking for what I just knew had to be a contract, I studied the pictures of Rock Hudson, Elizabeth

Taylor, and James Dean on the wall behind him. Gonna have to replace that one of Dean, I told myself.

About that time, Fred Guiol and Henry Ginsberg arrived. Fred looked like a mirror image of me, decked out in cowboy duds right down to his hat and boots. Tall and thin, he was a Randolph Scott–type character. Ginsberg looked like a stereotype of the Jewish movie executive: small, neatly dressed in a suit and tie. I found him to be quite the gentleman.

Mr. Stevens made the introductions, then said, "This is the guy I was telling you about."

The two men looked at me as if scrutinizing every detail: my leather-beaten face, my six-foot-plus frame, the way I carried myself. Then they nodded. The volume and the intensity level of my heartbeat kicked up a notch. *KA-THUMP KA-THUMP.* The anticipation was killing me. "Just give me the contract and let's get this rodeo on the road," I thought. Didn't say it, of course. I didn't want to appear too anxious. After all, that might cut the legs out from under my agent's negotiating position.

Mr. Stevens started to speak. In my mind, I already knew what the words would be: "Welcome aboard, Mr. Rink."

Funny thing, though, these are the words that actually came out: "Do you think you could teach Rock Hudson to talk like you do?"

I sat there for a moment, stunned, trying to process what I had heard. "You want to run that by me again?" I asked.

"Do you think you could teach Rock Hudson to talk like you do?"

"Mr. Stevens, to tell you the truth, I've been going to a speech coach to try to lose this damn accent."

All three men broke into laughter. I laughed with them, but damned if I knew what the hell was so funny.

"No, no, don't do that," Mr. Stevens said. "We want you to teach Rock to talk the way you do. We'll put you on the payroll as dialogue coach, and you'll work with the actors and be on the set every day. You'll have a job for the entire production."

My mind was busy wiping "Starring Robert Hinkle" off the slate. No Schwab's-Drugstore-discovery for me. No fame and fortune. No mansion in Beverly Hills. No signing autographs and adoring fans. But it was still a hell of an opportunity to be part of one of the biggest Hollywood productions in history.

"Well, how about it, Mr. Hinkle?"

"Hell yes, I can teach Rock Hudson to talk like a Texan."

George Stevens arranged for a limousine to take me directly to Universal International Studios to see Rock Hudson. Rock had made a number of movies, catapulted to stardom by his role opposite Jane Wyman in the remake of *Magnificent Obsession,* just as the same role had done two decades earlier for Robert Taylor. Now under contract at Universal, he was working on the story of Col. Dean Hess, called *Battle Hymn.*

Mr. Stevens's instructions were simple: "Just talk to him for a while and see what he thinks about your accent." In other words, go over there and be yourself. I believed I could handle that. I'd been handling it for twenty-four years.

I realized I had to adjust my thinking. Maybe I wasn't going to be Jett Rink and maybe I wasn't going to be a star, but things had still taken a turn for the better. I'd heard it said a hundred times that in Hollywood it's not what you know, it's who you know. In my few short years there, that had proven to be as true an adage as anything I had ever heard. I had gotten into my first movie purely by accident but stayed in the business because of people I knew.

A black limousine pulled up and the driver got out, wearing a black tuxedo topped off by a little black cap. I had never seen so much black. I headed for the door. The driver hustled toward me pretty fast, and my first thought was that I was about to get in somebody else's car. We did a little two-step until I figured out this was the right car, so I opened the door and got in. I found out later that the driver was going to open the door for me, but what did I know about limousine etiquette? Hell, if there was anything I could do, it was open my own car door.

I settled into the back seat, and the driver pulled away. I leaned deep into the plush leather and eyed the amenities, which included a small bar and a telephone for talking to the driver. Man, I felt like I was sittin' in high cotton! As we cruised through Toluca Lake toward Universal, I stared out the window at the beautiful houses with their well-manicured lawns. "One of these days," I told myself, "I'm gonna own one of them."

After we turned onto Lankershim Boulevard, we pulled up to the front gate in the middle of Universal Studios—the same gate where I had been unceremoniously turned away three years earlier until Chill Wills came to rescue me. But that's another story.

The driver rolled down his window as the guard approached. "We got Mr. Hinkle to see Mr. Hudson," the driver said.

There it was again: *Mister* Hinkle. I didn't think I had an ego back then, being merely a two-bit actor and stuntman in westerns, but that was starting to sound pretty good. And when the guard checked his clipboard and said, "Yes sir, take him to Stage Twenty-seven. Mr. Hudson is waiting," I thought I really sounded important. Mr. Hudson was waiting for *me.* No more turning away Bob Hinkle at the front gate. Boy, if my folks could see me now.

We pulled onto the lot, and the driver started wending his way to Stage 27, which was pretty far back on the lot, close to the western street sets. I'd worked there a few times in B westerns and TV shows, and I wondered if I'd see some of my cowboy buddies. I'd just wave at them as we drove by. I imagined the looks of shock on their faces, wondering what ol' Hinkle was doing in a limousine on the lot.

We drove past the studio cafeteria, Alfred Hitchcock's offices, a few dressing rooms, then past wardrobe and stopped in front of a big white warehouse-looking building that said

"Stage 27." A red light and a sign stood guard over the garage-type door, declaring "Do Not Enter When Light Is Flashing." Now experienced in the ways of limousine riding, I waited for the driver to open my door. If I was going to be a Hollywood limousine-riding big shot, I'd at least try to act like one. I was determined that this wasn't going to be my last limo ride.

The driver opened the stage door for me—man, I could get used to this—and we walked inside. The assistant director met us at the door. "Mr. Hinkle here to see Mr. Hudson," the driver said.

You never saw a production shut down so fast. The director, Douglas Sirk, stopped everything. A tall, good-looking guy dressed in a full colonel's U.S. Air Force uniform headed my way. It took me a minute to figure out that it was Rock. He had been expecting me, and I guess I must have looked about like he figured, standing there in my western clothes.

He greeted me as if we were old friends, then led me to his dressing room near the set. He picked up a copy of the *Giant* script that was lying on the desk, flipped over a few pages, pointed to a line of dialogue, and asked, "How would you say this?"

I looked at the script, then rattled it off in my now-good-as-gold Texas accent. Forget that speech coach. Talking like a Texan was starting to ring the cash register.

Rock listened as I spoke, then gave it a shot on his own. It wasn't bad, but it sounded more southern than Texan. "What do you think?" he asked.

"Well, a Texan wouldn't say it that way. You've got to drop your g's in the 'ing' words and bear down more on your r's." I gave him another sample of my good-as-gold Texas talk. I watched his face as he listened, taking in every nuance of not only my accent but also my pronunciation—flattening my a's, rounding my o's, and dropping my g's. "Barbed wire" became "bob wahr," "oil business" became "awl bidness," "fire" became "far." One syllable became two, and two almost became separate words—"guitar" became "gui-tar" and "po-lice" became "po-lice." The cadence slows lazily. Texans don't just say the words; they linger over them like they're old friends, worthy of a cup of coffee. It's the journey, not the destination, that's important in a conversation.

Rock nodded, excitement working its way onto his face. He gave it another stab or two, and I was amazed at how quickly he picked things up. It wasn't long until he had moved closer to Texas. He was not quite there yet, maybe in Arizona or western New Mexico, but definitely out of Hollywood.

After we talked for a bit, he called George Stevens on the phone. "George, this will be perfect. I really like this." And I could see that he meant it.

After he hung up he said, "George wants to see you in his office."

He walked me to the limousine, where he shook my hand and we said good-bye. I settled into the limo, unable to keep a self-satisfied smile from my face. I knew I had just been tested, and I knew I had aced the exam.

Texas Bob Hinkle had arrived on *Giant*.

"Think you can turn him into a Texan?" George asked when I got back to his office.

"He picks it up pretty quick. Besides, he's tall and good-looking—just like most of us Texans."

George nearly busted a gut over that one, but I didn't think it was so funny. No brag, just fact.

"I think you're gonna be all right," he said, then he closed our meeting with a bit of business. "Go down to the personnel office and give them your Social Security number, your address, and anything else they need. You've already been on salary all day."

About that: just what was my salary going to be?

"When you work as an actor, how much do you make?" he asked, as if reading my mind.

That was a hell of a question because it left room to maneuver. There's what I typically made when I worked; there's the average of what I made, taking into account all the days I didn't work; and there's that five hundred dollars I once made for a week's work. That last number sounded pretty good to me, even if it had been for only one week. He didn't have to know that, though. I figured it was a good starting point for negotiating.

"Well, I made five hundred dollars over there at Paramount," I said.

He chewed on that for a moment, then nodded. I geared myself for his counter. "Well, that's what I'm going to give you over here," he said. "Five hundred a week sound okay?"

Damn right it did! I knew the picture was going to run six or seven months, and at five hundred dollars a week I'd make more in half a year than I normally made in two years. I hoped I seemed calm on the outside, but on the inside my emotions were on a wild bull ride. "Yes sir, that's just fine with me."

He turned to his secretary. "We need to set up an office for Mr. Hinkle. Find out if Alan Ladd's dressing room is occupied."

Alan Ladd? Old Shane himself? Yep, that sounded mighty fine to me, too. Not only was his dressing room one of the biggest and best on the lot, but I had been a big fan of his ever since I first saw *Shane*. It seemed as if things just couldn't get any better for this old cowboy.

Alan Ladd's dressing room was everything I had hoped it would be. Located in a bungalow one street left of the main entrance, just down a ways from George Stevens's office, it was more of a guesthouse than a dressing room. There was a small bedroom with a double bed, a good-sized living room that could be fixed up to seat eight or ten people, a bathroom, and a tiny kitchen. A desk had been set up in the living room. About the time I got there, some guy from the prop department brought in a tape recorder, legal pads, pens, and pencils—everything a good dialogue coach would need. I even got a pass to drive onto the lot. Can you believe that? All I had to do was drive up to the gate, and they'd wave me right on in.

As soon as I had the office set up, I called my wife, Sandy. She had just delivered our second son, Brad, on February 28—just one day after Elizabeth Taylor gave birth to her second child, Chris—and was still not feeling well. It had been a particularly difficult delivery, and I thought this bit of good news might cheer her up.

"You're not going to believe where I am," I said.

"Tell me."

"In my own Warner Brothers office, right here in Alan Ladd's old dressing room."

I could almost hear the life flow back into her voice when she responded. "When do I get to come down there? You'll have to take me on a tour. We can even have lunch in the Green Room."

It was good to hear that excitement in her voice. After all, we were in this together.

After I hung up, there was one more thing I had to do. I picked up the phone again and dialed a number.

"Warner Brothers Studio," the switchboard operator said.

"I need to talk to Bob Hinkle," I said.

"One minute, please."

She put me on hold for a few seconds, then came back on the line. "I'm sorry, but Mr. Hinkle's extension is busy. Would you like to wait?"

"No ma'am, I'll try back later."

I hung up the phone and sat there, not bothering to fight the idiot grin on my face. Yep, not only was Bob Hinkle on the lot, they *knew* Bob Hinkle was on the lot. That meant Bob Hinkle *belonged* on the lot. I'll say it again: it was a long way from Brownfield, Texas, to Hollywood, California.

But how in the hell did I get there?

CHAPTER TWO

The Sky's the Limit

When you take those sharp turns at low speed like that, it can
throw you into a spin right into the damn ground.

—B. W. YOUNG, FLIGHT INSTRUCTOR

I suppose I could have been a pilot. After all, I soloed in a
Piper J3 Cub on my sixteenth birthday with only seven
hours and five minutes of instruction under my belt. How
many sixteen-year-olds do that?

Oh yeah, I also got grounded the same day.

It happened in my west Texas hometown of Brownfield,
county seat of Terry County. Dang near spitting distance from
Lubbock, Brownfield has turned out some notables, including
Texas Tech basketball All-American and WNBA superstar Sheryl Swoopes; light heavyweight Golden Gloves boxing champion Tom Adams; Texas Tech football All-American Jerrell
Price, who later became owner and chief chef of the popular 50
Yard Line Restaurant in Lubbock; and the ambassador of Texas
music, Gary P. Nunn. Sheryl could shoot the lights out of any
gym in the country. Tom actually won five Golden Gloves titles
in Texas. Jerrell went on to play in the NFL, but most west Texans remember him for his steaks at the 50 Yard Line. And Gary?
Well, what Texan doesn't know by heart the chorus to "London
Homesick Blues," about "going home with the armadillos."

Well, that's Brownfield: armadillos, country music,
friendly people—and miles and miles of cotton fields on the

flattest land you've ever seen. On a clear day, if you look real hard, you can see the back of your head. And dry? Some days were so dry you could spit cotton. The funny thing was, it could also flood. We didn't get much rain, but when we did, it was usually a gully washer. Because the land was so flat, there was nowhere for the water to run off. One time I saw folks planting cotton out of a motorboat. Another time, an ol' boy had to go down twelve feet to grease a windmill. Okay, maybe that's a couple of Texas tall tales, but I think you get my drift.

When I was growing up, Brownfield consisted of about ten thousand good, decent folks—and an SOB or two, but what town didn't have its share of those? Both my parents were working people. My dad worked at the chemical plant, and my mother ran a hotel in town called the Wines Hotel. At lunchtime, they served family-style meals to the local merchants. For thirty-five cents they could eat all they wanted—chicken fried steak, mashed potatoes, beans, and iced tea, all west Texas staples.

I was the eldest of three kids. Next came my brother, Dink (believe it or not, he preferred that to Eugene), then my sister, Leta. When I was fourteen we got indoor plumbing, and I was finally able to take baths in a real bathtub instead of a metal washtub. We were so poor we could only afford a tumbleweed for a pet, and Dink and I had to ride double on a stick horse. It wasn't until I moved to Hollywood and started making decent money that I got my first glimpse of how the silk stocking folks lived. I used to joke that I moved to California for my health—to keep from starving to death—and that they'd have to whitewash our house in Brownfield before they could condemn it, but it was a good life growing up. I had everything I needed.

I've got no complaints.

On July 25, 1946, the day I turned sixteen, B. W. Young, my flying instructor at Triangle Airport just outside the city limits, was going to let me solo for the first time. Gene Patterson, Joe Dale Scott, R. J. Riley, and I piled into my dad's 1940 Chevrolet—I don't believe he ever owned a new car, but this one had been stored in a barn for most of the war, so it was almost like new—and headed to the airport. As I climbed out I told Gene, "When I take off, y'all head to Maurice's house, and I'll meet you there." Maurice Martin lived four or five miles away on a farm near a little place called Gomez. It was all dry-land farming back then, mostly cotton and maize, with irrigation still a year or two in the future. I figured I could put on a show for the boys over those fields.

I went to the Piper Cub J3, which was about the smallest plane you could get at the time, and climbed inside. B.W. and a couple of other pilots watched me take off, probably ready to criticize everything the young whippersnapper did or to come to my rescue if I flamed out. I cranked up the engine, then taxied down the dirt runway, gaining speed all the while. Gene and the other boys left in Dad's car about the same time I went airborne.

Although I had never soloed before, I was too young and arrogant to be nervous or scared. I don't know if it was just the Texan in me—like they say, never ask a man if he's from Texas; if he is, he'll tell you and if he's not, no reason to embarrass him—but I was as comfortable flying that plane all by my lonesome as I would have been driving Dad's car.

I leveled off at about a thousand feet and started looking for the boys. Sure enough, there they were on the highway, cutting through fields of cotton and maize. It was time to start the show. I dropped to about thirty feet, parallel to the highway, and flew beside them for a while. I didn't have to worry about the high-line wires because they ran parallel to the highway on the other side, but every now and then I came to telephone wires that peeled off perpendicular to farmhouses, so I'd hop up and over, then back down again. I could see the ol' boys in the car, laughing and pointing.

I came to another telephone wire, but this one didn't have a barbed wire fence beneath it, which gave it a bit more clearance. Hmmm. Wonder if I can fly *under* it?

Let's find out.

I pushed forward on the stick, and the nose of the plane dipped. I held it on an angle and swooped to ten feet or less off the ground, leveled off, and went right under the wire. The wheels hung down about two feet from the bottom of the fuselage, and I could hear the tops of the maize slapping them. I knew I must have really been tickling my buddies to death. They were probably saying, "Boy, look at Bobby. Can't he fly!"

Well, they hadn't seen anything from ol' Bobby Hinkle yet. When I got to Maurice's daddy's land, I really put on an air show. I climbed to about three thousand feet, did a two- or three-turn spin, and came out of it into a loop. I did every stunt I'd learned: spins, dives, you name it. I should have charged them for that show.

When I got back to the airport, B.W. and a couple of the other guys were waiting. I figured they wanted to congratulate me on the trick flying, a lot of which was visible from the airport. I landed smoothly, cut the engine, and hopped out, all smiles.

"Bobby, I didn't think you'd do it," B.W. said.

I might not have been the sharpest knife in the drawer, but I knew from his tone that I was in trouble. Only one way to handle it: play dumb. Some might have said I wasn't playing.

"Do what?"

"We've been watching you diving all over the place, just waiting for you to plow into the ground. Don't you know how dangerous that is?"

I guess I did, but he cleared it up in case there was any confusion.

"When you take those sharp turns at low speed like that, it can throw you into a spin right into the damn ground."

I didn't know if he was worried about me or about his airplane, but he made his case pretty emphatically. Now if he'd just shut up and let me go on my way.

"You're grounded. No more flying for a week."

No words could have crushed my spirit more. I'd built up a couple of hours of free flying time by working at the airport, and I hadn't used more than forty-five minutes before I got grounded.

But don't cry for me. It was all going to pay off later.

In the spring of 1947, B. W. Young bought six Stearman biplanes from an airbase in Hobbs, New Mexico, about seventy miles west of Brownfield. The planes had two seats, front and back, and 220-horsepower Continental engines. B.W.'s plan was to convert them to crop dusters, putting in 450-hp Pratt and Whitney engines for the power needed to haul fertilizer. But first he had to retrieve them from Hobbs.

"You think you could fly one of them?" he asked.

I'd never flown one, never even seen one, but I had already learned something that would stand me in good stead the rest of my career: guts and BS often make up for lack of experience.

"Hell yeah," I said, as if he'd just asked the stupidest question in the world.

So we hopped a bus to Hobbs, where the seller picked us up at the bus station and drove us to the airbase. And there they were: six Stearman biplanes lined up on the first runway, silver finish glinting in the sunlight. I couldn't wait to get into the cockpit of one of those suckers.

Since neither B.W. nor I had ever flown these planes, we needed some instruction. I went ahead of B.W., and the flight instructor showed me some things I needed to know. I took mental notes of everything he said, then made two or three landings—real smooth, if I do say so myself. He must have thought so, too, because he cut me loose to fly the first plane back to Texas.

Well, funny thing, since B.W. had so many hours in small planes, he wasn't accustomed to learning instead of teaching. I had applied one of those little helpful hints I learned in west Texas—never miss a chance to shut up—so I was way ahead of B.W. He was used to flying J3 Cubs, which were like cars without power steering, but the Stearmans had ball-bearing controls that made them easier to control. If you weren't used to it, you could easily overcompensate. That could cause all kinds of problems—just like it did for B.W.

I ended up flying all the planes to Brownfield except one. By the time I was on my fifth, I was an old pro. And I hadn't learned a thing since showing off for the boys at Maurice's. As I was flying the fifth plane back to Brownfield, I spotted a tractor in a field heading away from me as I crossed from New Mexico into Texas. I doubted if he could hear me over his tractor.

I slipped up behind him as close as I could, then went into a dive. I don't know if he sensed me first or finally heard me, but he swung his head around, eyes about to bug out. He must have thought the Japanese had struck again but missed Pearl Harbor and ended up in west Texas. Just as I swooped over him he bailed out, hit the dirt, and came up running. His tractor kept rolling a bit more, then veered across a couple of rows of plowed field and finally stopped. I knew he must have been cussing a blue streak at me, but I didn't care. Yes sir, I was meant to fly.

Over time, I learned to fly just about everything they brought to that little airport, including a Cessna UC78, known as a Bamboo Bomber. One day a couple of U.S. Air Force pilots showed up and wanted to rent planes. They were in advanced training at Reese Air Force Base near Lubbock, so I knew they could fly, but I wanted to see what they had.

"I'll have to ride around the patch a couple of times with you first, on account of our insurance," I said. So I got in a Stearman with one of them, and we took off. He got about five feet off the ground as we approached the end of the runway, then he showed me what real flying was. He pulled around to the left in a constant turn from one end of the airport to the other, a maneuver called a shondell. Then he swung back around to the runway and landed, all in one smooth move. Man, it was beautiful!

For the next couple of hours I was in heaven as I watched them fly. They started side by side, rolling down the runway, then took off in formation. After that, they did just about every acrobatic move in the book: loops, slow rolls, snap rolls, spins, you name it. A couple of weeks later, one of them came back and taught me some of those tricks. After that, I was totally spoiled for plain old flying.

It may not seem like it, but my flying experiences were the first steps toward my career in Hollywood. The next step came when my love of flying led me to air force recruiters before my senior year of high school. I was tired of school, so I signed up in November 1947. I didn't totally give up on school, though. I almost immediately began taking correspondence courses to get my GED and actually graduated with my class the next year.

In June 1948, the Berlin Airlift started. The Russians were trying to take control over the entire city of Berlin, which was located in the eastern half of Germany given to them when the country was divided after World War II. They blocked all railroad and street access into the western sectors of the city, which had been given to the Allies, effectively giving the Russians total control. The Americans and British organized a supply train to end all supply trains, ultimately flying over five thousand tons of food and supplies per day into West Berlin for almost a year before the Russians blinked.

Near the end of 1948, I was stationed at Fourth Head-quarters at Hamilton Air Force Base, near San Francisco. The commander, Colonel R. J. Vandergriff, liked me, so he made me the crew chief on a long-range military transport plane, called a C-47, that had been assigned to him. The air force was testing pilots and crew chiefs to help out with the airlift because they needed to dramatically increase the tonnage they were flying daily, making it an "all hands on deck" kind of deal. When the call went out, I answered.

The air force sent me overseas, and I spent the next few months as crew chief on flights carrying coal into Berlin. At first, I was on a C-47, but with just two engines those planes couldn't handle the volume that was needed, so they switched us to C-54s, which had four engines. During the air-lift, five levels of planes flew into Berlin at three-minute intervals, following specific routes. We got only one pass at landing, and if we missed it we had to return fully loaded and get in line for our next run. Heavy, low-lying fog wasn't uncommon, and on more than one occasion we burst beneath the fog as we were landing, only to find that we were as much as five hundred feet closer to the ground than we thought. That's pretty dicey when you're loaded with coal and dropping fast.

Once we landed, my job was to make sure the plane was emptied in less than thirty minutes. The coal was in forty-pound gunnysacks, and my crew would load them onto a conveyor belt, while another crew on the ground would unload them into a waiting truck. We usually had about three truck-loads on each flight. I developed a system that involved rotating the men in their positions on the belt, which not only sped up the process but also kept the men fresher. The air force even had me spend three days training other crews on this process. It must have worked because I've heard that one twelve-man crew set a record by unloading ten tons of coal in under six minutes.

We never knew whether the Russians were going to try to shoot us down. Sometimes they'd fly alongside in armed planes, just so we'd know they were there. Now, that was plumb exciting, and the adrenaline pumped for all it was worth. It felt a lot like riding bulls, only the stakes were higher. On one flight, our co-pilot had a heart attack about halfway to Berlin from Frankfort. Back in the hold of the plane, we got a frantic request from the pilot: "Has anybody had any experience flying?"

"I have," I said. I didn't bother to explain that I had never flown a C-54. I'd never driven a Rolls Royce either, but I figured it wasn't a whole lot different than driving Dad's Chevrolet. And I figured an airplane was still an airplane. Besides, remember what I said before about guts and BS?

"Get over there in that seat," the pilot said. When we got to Berlin, a doctor came onboard to check out our stricken co-pilot while we unloaded. Fortunately, it wasn't a serious heart attack, and he was able to return to the United States to recover, but I co-piloted that flight the rest of the way to Berlin and back to Frankfort after we unloaded.

All told, I spent seven-and-a-half months, with six months of actual flying, as part of the airlift. None of my flights ever brought in food, as we were strictly coal transport. We did follow the lead, though, of another American pilot who started dropping candy to the German kids. We'd go to supply and get torn sheets and make parachutes out of them, then we'd pool our money and buy boxes of candy at the PX—Baby Ruth, Butterfinger, Hershey's, Three Musketeers, every kind imaginable—and drop them over fields where the kids waited. One of the great thrills of my life was seeing as many as five hundred kids scrambling for that candy. Their dentists might not have liked it, but it was one of the greatest U.S. public relations coups of all time.

And the airlift as a whole was a remarkable testament to the U.S. military and the American work ethic.

CHAPTER THREE

Breaking into Hollywood

I'm gonna ride this ol' bull for you, and then I'm gonna take
you to the dance after this is over.

—BOB HINKLE

I transferred back to the States in July 1949. My folks had
moved to Portland, Oregon, so I asked to be near them.
Larson Air Force Base at Moses Lake, Washington, and another base near Tacoma were the closest available locations
to Portland. A friend from Brownfield named Joe Hill had
moved to Moses Lake where his dad opened what we now
know as a Laundromat; back then, they were just called laun-
dries. So Moses Lake seemed like a good fit.

I never would have guessed it, with Washington so far from
Texas, but it was a hotbed of rodeo activity. I had free time on
the weekends, so I rodeoed while I was still in the service. I did
pretty well, winning more than I spent, so how could I com-
plain? I started with bull riding because you didn't need much
equipment, just a pair of spurs and a bull rope. For bareback
riding, you also needed a pair of chaps and a bareback rigging.
I'd been calf roping ever since I was a little bitty kid, but you
needed a horse, and I didn't have enough money to buy one.

I was a sergeant by then, making probably $125 or $130 a
month from the air force, plus my room, board, and medical,
so everything I won rodeoing was gravy. I didn't win many

firsts, but I did win a lot of thirds or fourths in bull riding, which usually paid about 60 or 70 bucks per win. I wasn't getting rich by any means, but I saved enough to buy a quarter horse named Wink that I trained myself. After that I pretty much, but not completely, gave up bareback riding and bull riding and stuck to calf roping and bulldogging. It wasn't much of a sacrifice; I wasn't that good at the former.

My real stroke of luck came in September 1950, after I was discharged from the service. That was when I first met Sandra Larson, queen of the rodeo in Moses Lake. My folks had moved there from Portland, so I was living with them. I was working construction, making two dollars an hour in a booming industry and saving as much money as I could. I had seen Sandra at the rodeo, messing with the horses, and I couldn't take my eyes off her. She wasn't much of a horseman, but she was by far the prettiest girl in town. I could tell right away that she was a classy lady. She knew how to wear makeup without overdoing it, and she knew how to dress up.

The first time I talked to her was nearly my last. I caught a whiff of her perfume one day and said, "Boy, you smell as good as a new saddle." She wasn't sure how to take that, but if you've ever smelled a new saddle, you know that's about the ultimate compliment a cowboy can pay a girl.

I'd had my eye on Sandra for a while before I finally decided to make my move at one of the weekend rodeos. I told Gerald Roberts, the 1948 World Champion All-Around Rodeo Cowboy, "I sure would like to go on a date with her."

"She'd never go with you. She's one of them good girls, and they don't think much of cowboys who chew tobacco and drink beer."

I tossed away my beer can, spit out my chaw, and stuck out my hand. "Twenty dollars says I can get a date with her."

"You're on."

I saw my chance when it came time for the bull ride. She was in the announcer's stand, just above the bull chute. When my turn came, I crawled on my bull and looked right at her. She looked back, and my legs just about turned to rubber. I mustered all the courage I had and said, "I'm gonna ride this ol' bull for you, and then I'm gonna take you to the dance after this is over."

She kind of smiled, or maybe it was a look of pity. I reckon I probably wasn't the first cowboy to say something like that to her, but I aimed to be the last.

I grabbed hold of the rope and wrapped it around my hand, then I slapped the bull on his hump, just to tick him off. That sucker hit the end of the chute so hard it shook the announcer's stand. It accomplished my purpose because she really was watching me then to see whether she needed to worry about my threat to take her to the dance.

The chute opened, and that big old Brahma bull bucked straight up and out in one smooth motion. He had good altitude, but he never twisted or turned back, and that made it an easy ride. Eight seconds later, the whistle blew. I stepped off and landed on my feet, as if I'd planned it that way. I tipped my hat to her, and she smiled—a real smile this time.

I got a good score because I'd made the time and landed on my feet—style points, I guess. Everybody gave me a pretty good ovation while I walked into the stands, my attention set on the rodeo queen. I made my way to where she was sitting. She looked at me for a second, then scooted over and I sat down. By the time the rodeo was over, I had talked her into going to the dance with me, and next thing you know, we were going steady. After that, the only time we were apart was when she went back to Brigham Young University to finish college and I went back to Texas to work in the oilfields for the winter.

We got married in June 1952. And this ol' cowboy is still married to the rodeo queen of Moses Lake, Washington—still dancing with the one who brung him.

I suppose you're wondering where all this is headed and what it's got to do with my getting into the movie business. Well, I'm getting there, but the getting there's as important as the being there.

In September 1952 I entered a rodeo in Pendleton, Oregon. As luck would have it, director Budd Boetticher* was shooting a movie in Hollywood about rodeo life, called *Bronco Buster*, starring Scott Brady and John Lund. Brady was still pretty new in the movie business, but he would go on to a long career with plenty of television and movie credits, including a number of episodes of *The Rockford Files*. Lund was already fairly well established and was an officer in the Screen Actors Guild.

One of the supporting players who played a rodeo clown was a Texas boy named Chill Wills, from a Dallas suburb called Seagoville. Budd brought Chill and his second unit to Pendleton to shoot rodeo footage for *Bronco Buster*. I was the general size of one of the stars, so they dressed me in western clothes to match the character's wardrobe in the movie. All I had to do for my three hundred dollars a day was what I was doing anyway—ride rodeo.

When Budd packed up his crew to go back to Hollywood, he said, "When you finish up the rodeo this year, if you get a chance, come by Hollywood and look me up. I might have something for you."

That sounded an awful lot like one of those "let's get togethers" at some uncertain time in the future that we all know don't mean a thing, so I wrote the whole experience off as a

---

*Boetticher had his own Texas connection: he had directed World War II hero Audie Murphy, from Farmersville, Texas (or Greenville, the other Texas town vying to be Murphy's official "hometown"), in *The Cimarron Kid*. He would later direct a number of episodes of various television shows such as *The Public Defender, Maverick, 77 Sunset Strip,* and *The Rifleman.*

bit of high-paying fun. But when I finished the rodeo season, that three hundred dollars a day I got on *Bronco Buster* settled in the front of my brain and took up residence. Sandy and I talked about it and figured we could at least give Hollywood a try. What could it hurt?

Sometime after Halloween 1952, we hit Los Angeles and rented a house on Ventura Boulevard near Republic Pictures. Republic had cut its nut making B westerns with such stars as Gene Autry, Roy Rogers, and John Wayne. That stint on *Bronco Buster* was like a shot straight into the main line, so even though I found a job doing carpentry to pay the bills, I focused my efforts on figuring out how to break into the picture business.

There was a restaurant near our house—right across the street from Republic's front gate—called the Back Stage, where a lot of the extras and stuntmen working in the westerns would spend time during breaks in shooting. I noticed that when they went back to work, the guard at the gate let them walk right on through. Since they were all dressed in western attire and I had my own *real* western wardrobe, I thought I could probably blend in pretty well. They'd probably think I was a new extra and not pay me any mind. At least that's what I hoped.

So one day I put on my western gear and waited for a group to head back across the street. Sure enough, the guard didn't say a word, and I followed the others into the studio. I spent the rest of the day wandering around the sets. That worked so well that I did it again the next day. This time an ol' boy named Cap Somers, who did stunts and extra work in a lot of movies and television shows, struck up a conversation.

"If you want to get into the picture business," he told me, "you need to get an 'extra' card so you can get some work on these movies. Then, if they've got a stunt, volunteer for it, or if they've got a bit part, they may give you that."

Following Cap's advice, I went to Central Casting and tried to get registered as an extra, but they told me they weren't taking anybody new. After about a month or so of trying, I was totally frustrated. I was this close to the movies, but I couldn't get in. Budd Boetticher had told me to look him up, but I didn't think he really meant it. Still, desperate times require desperate acts, so I started asking around about him. I finally got word that he was shooting a picture at Universal Studios. Not knowing any better, I drove to Universal, parked outside, then headed toward the front gate as if I were going to walk right in.

The guard stopped me. "Is your name on the list, sir?"

List? What list? "I'm going to see Budd Boetticher. I'm a friend of his."

"Your name's not on the list, so I can't let you in."

"I won't be long. I just need to get his phone number."

"Seems like if you were a friend of his, you'd already have his number."

I had to admit he had a point, but he just didn't understand Texans. You howdy and shake hands with a fellow, do a little rodeoing for his movie, and damned if that doesn't make you friends—phone number or not. How do you explain that to someone from California?

"Hey, Hollywood!"

I knew that voice. Sure enough, there was Chill Wills, pulling up to the gate in his white El Dorado Cadillac. He had the top down and wore his custom-made hundred-dollar Stetson. "What are you doing here?" he asked.

"I'm trying to get in to see Budd."

"Well, get in this Cadillac and let's go find him."

I hopped in, and he drove through the gate with a wave and smile at the guard.

"I guess they know you," I said.

"They ought to," Chill said. "I'm in and out of here all the time. I'm the voice of Francis, the talking mule." Then, before that could sink in, he added, "Let's get some lunch."

I was born with a hollow leg and could always eat, so we went to the studio cafeteria and grabbed a quick bite. I filled Chill in on what I'd been doing, then I said, "Budd told me to look him up if I ever got down this way. He said he might have something for me in the movies. I heard he was doing a picture here."

"I'll see if I can find out where."

Chill seemed to know just about everyone on the lot, which I guess isn't that surprising for Francis, the talking mule. It might also have had something to do with the fact that he'd been in the business for nearly twenty years and had over sixty credits under his belt. I was looking forward to the day when I would have all those credits and know all those folks.

He made a few inquiries and, sure enough, Budd was making a movie on the back lot called *Wings of the Hawk,* with Van Heflin, Julie Adams, and Noah Beery, Jr. I was full of anticipation as Chill drove past sound stages and familiar street scenery I had seen in movies and on TV. I figured one of two things was about to happen when we got to Budd's set: either he wouldn't remember me and would send me packing, or he really meant what he said, and I'd be on my way.

We found Budd on the western street on the back lot, where he and Julie Adams were sitting under a tree, talking.

"Hey Budd, look who I found," Chill said. "One of them old cowboys from up there at Pendleton."

"Hi, Budd, I'm Bob Hinkle," I said quickly, before he could wonder who the hell I was. "How you doing?"

"Doing good, Bob. What are you doing here?"

Okay, maybe there were three possibilities of what could happen, the third being he'd know who I was but forget he'd invited me down. Time to find out.

"Well, I thought maybe I'd get in the pictures." I might even have toed the ground with my boot and "aw shucksed" a time or two.

Budd didn't hesitate. He called his assistant director over and said, "Get Bob in here tomorrow. I'm going to use him in a scene."

And just like that, I was in the picture business. I got killed the next day on *Wings of the Hawk*, gunned down by a machine gun. My mother cried later when she saw me die in my first movie. From then on, I did just about everything I could to get noticed, mostly a lot of extra work and stunts that usually involved falling down. Hell, I'd been falling down since I was a kid, so there was nothing to that. I progressed to other, more difficult stunts, but they were nothing a rodeo cowboy couldn't handle.

I ultimately got my guild cards, thanks in no small part to a letter written to Central Casting on my behalf by Bill Elliott, better known in the picture business as Wild Bill Elliott. He started in the business in 1925, so he was a veteran of over twenty-five years by the time I showed up on the studio lots, and he had no reason to help a young kid like me other than the fact that he was a decent man. His credits included a slew of B westerns, including a series of pictures in which he starred as the character Wild Bill Saunders, thus earning his nickname. Following the theme, he went on to play Wild Bill Hickok in movies such as *The Wildcat of Tucson* and *Hands across the Rockies*, then starred in a series playing a character named Wild Bill Elliott, followed by a series playing Red Ryder.

On November 23, 1952, he wrote a letter to Bert Dakin at Central Casting that said:

Dear Sir:

Bob Hinkle has just moved from Texas to California where he intends to make his home and is very anxious to secure cards in the Screen Extras Guild and the Screen Actors Guild.

For the past three years I have been producing rodeo's [*sic*] in the southwest and Bob has contested in

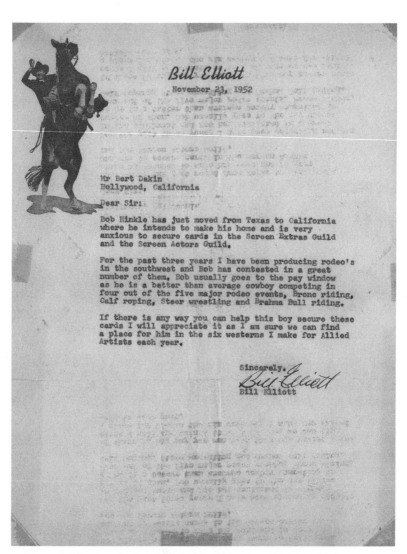

Bill Elliott

November 23, 1952

Mr Bert Dakin
Hollywood, California

Dear Sir:

Bob Hinkle has just moved from Texas to California
where he intends to make his home and is very
anxious to secure cards in the Screen Extras Guild
and the Screen Actors Guild.

For the past three years I have been producing rodeo's
in the southwest and Bob has contested in a great
number of them. Bob usually goes to the pay window
as he is a better than average cowboy competing in
four out of the five major rodeo events, Bronc riding,
Calf roping, Steer wrestling and Brahma Bull riding.

If there is any way you can help this boy secure these
cards I will appreciate it as I am sure we can find
a place for him in the six westerns I make for Allied
Artists each year.

Sincerely,

Bill Elliott

Letter to Bert Dakin from Bill Elliott. Courtesy of Bob Hinkle.

On the set of *Men of the Fighting Lady* (1954). *Left to right:* Paul Smith, Mike Coughlin, Bob, and Frank Lovejoy. © 1954 Loew's Inc.

a great number of them. Bob usually goes to the pay window as he is a better than average cowboy competing in four out of the five major rodeo events, Bronc riding, Calf roping, Steer wrestling and Brahma Bull riding.

If there is any way you can help this boy secure these cards I will appreciate it as I am sure we can find a place for him in the six westerns I make for Allied Artists each year.

     Sincerely,
     Bill Elliott

Universal Studios was about a mile down toward Ventura Boulevard, on Lankershim, from our house. Beyond that was Warner Brothers, and in between, off of Barham, was Columbia

The Making of *Giant*

CHAPTER FOUR

Rebel Without an Accent

I want to be a Texan, twenty-four hours a day.

—James Dean

I woke up that first morning after George Stevens hired me, wondering if it had been a dream. But when I showed up at Warner Brothers and Alan Ladd's dressing room was still my office, I knew it was real.

About nine o'clock, George called me over for my first assignment as dialogue coach. When I arrived, George treated me as if we were old buddies who'd known each other for years, not just days. He had that way about him. I discovered that he was as much psychologist as he was movie director. In fact, George never acted like I was hired help. After our initial meeting, he treated me no differently than he did Rock Hudson or Elizabeth Taylor. Or even Jack Warner, the head of the studio. Any time I saw him, he was always ready with a greeting: "Hey Bob, how ya doing?" He fit right in when we got to Marfa with his down-home, Texas-style hospitality.

I remember one time while we were shooting in Marfa, he joined Jimmy Dean and me for dinner at the Paisano Hotel. After dinner, Jimmy went back to where he was staying, and George said, "Bob, let's take a walk."

We headed toward the courthouse square, about a block away. He put his arm around my shoulder, like he might with his son or a buddy. I've got to tell you, it kinda shook me up at the time. I'd heard all kinds of stories about the—to use modern terms—"alternative lifestyle" of some folks in Holly-wood. That was a bit foreign to an ol' boy from west Texas. I thought to myself, "Oh Lord, here it comes. How am I gonna get out of this?"

But my fears were misplaced. George was just concerned about how I was getting along on the film since I was some-what of an outsider. "Everybody treating you all right?" he asked. "Any problems I need to know about?" He went down the list of the actors, wanting to know how they were coming with their transformation into Texans and whether the wardrobe looked authentic. He asked my opinion about a lot of things involving the production. I found out later that I was close to the same age as his son, George, Jr. I think he missed him, so he was looking after me, almost as if I were an orphan. It made me feel right at home.

But back to the day after he hired me. When I got to George's office he asked, "Do you know who Mercedes McCambridge is?"

I knew of her from various television shows she'd been in. And who could forget movies like *All the King's Men*, for which she had won an Oscar and a Golden Globe for best support-ing actress, and the previous year's *Johnny Guitar*, with Ster-ling Hayden and Joan Crawford? Having names like hers even come up in conversation was a thrill for me, never mind what I knew was bound to be coming next: I was about to be asked to work with her.

"Well," George said, "I've been thinking about her for the part of Luz—that's Rock's sister in the movie. Do you think she could play that part?"

"Man, I don't know." That wasn't the kind of answer to in-spire confidence in my abilities, but I had a hard time believ-ing he was really asking me to help with a casting decision. I went out on a limb. "She's a good actress. I think she could play any kind of a part."

"She has a tendency sometimes to overdo it. I want her to be a pure Texan, and I don't want her to get in there and go all syrupy sweet on me, you know, like she's from the South."

I knew George had more than just accent concerns. Like I said, who could forget *Johnny Guitar* and the rumors of Mercedes's clash with Joan Crawford, who was reportedly jealous of Mercedes and her popularity with the rest of the cast and crew? Rumor had it that at the end of filming one day, Joan waited until everyone had gone home and tore Mercedes's costume to shreds. That delayed everything the next day until wardrobe could replace her costume. Joan apparently hoped the crew would blame Mercedes, as if she could elevate her own popularity by damaging someone else's. I'd even heard that the director of the movie, Nicholas Ray, was so upset by the way the two stars clashed that he threw up every morning before going to the set. I knew what George was thinking: what would happen when Mercedes and Elizabeth Taylor got together?

"Take your tape recorder and go to her house," he said. "I want you to tape that scene out on the roundup where Luz lays down the law to Bick about it being her house after he brings Leslie home." Leslie was the role to be played by Elizabeth Taylor. "Bring the tape back and let's talk about it."

I was anxious to prove my worth to George, so I jumped in my car—no more limo services; that was just to set the hook—and drove to Beverly Hills, where Mercedes lived in a beautiful two-story home that sat on about a half-acre. I don't know if George had given her any special instructions about me, but she treated me extra nice, almost as if I were an extension of George himself. I got the impression she thought I might have some say in whether she got the part. I'm not saying she was phony, just that she didn't seem resentful of the things I asked her to do. A lot of actors wouldn't have been so gracious to some joker from west Texas who had almost nothing to do with the picture business other than falling down a lot on TV westerns and who suddenly showed up at their door with a tape recorder and started making demands.

But not Mercedes. She welcomed me into her home and led me to a big living room, where I saw that she had a script, with pencil marks on it, on the coffee table. I guess she had been making notes about the character and how to play her. I would have given anything to know what they were. Off to the side was a huge dining room, with a table that looked like it could seat a dozen people. I don't know how many bedrooms or baths the house had, but my family back in Brownfield could easily have lived in just the bottom floor and still had room for company.

Mercedes asked her housekeeper to fix lunch, and we chatted over tuna sandwiches. She seemed genuinely interested in my background as a rodeo cowboy and in Texas in general. I'd noticed that Texas and Texans were curiosities of a sort in Hollywood, which made me one as well. I found myself mostly answering questions and not asking many of my own.

After we ate, it was time to get to work. I had my own copy of the script and she had hers, so we turned to the scene George wanted us to record. I read Rock's part as Bick while she read Luz's role. We rocked along for a bit, then all of a sudden she barked at me on one of the lines, like Luz does to Bick in the movie. Now, I don't scare or intimidate easily, but she got my attention stronger than some of the bulls I had ridden. I thought we were just recording her stab at a Texas accent, but she didn't hold anything back. Instead of just reading, she was *acting*. She really got into the character of Luz and ripped into Bick, just as she would later do in the movie. I found myself almost feeling sorry for ol' Rock.

We played it back and listened to how it sounded. As good as her acting was, there was room for improvement in talking like a Texan. Maybe I had something to offer after all.

"When you said 'I know how to handle Mex-i-cans,'" I said, "you pronounced all the syllables. But in Texas we say 'Mes-kins.'"

She thought about that for a second, then nodded.

"See," I went on, "they're *your* people. The Reata is *your* ranch and the folks that work there are *yours*. It's like you own them. Not like slaves or anything, because they get paid, but in your mind they're yours. And you talk about 'em that way."

We went through it again, and this time she really laid it on. She picked up things fast, and that made me feel good. I wasn't used to teaching people how to talk or use accents, so I was pretty much flying by the seat of my pants. She was a good observer, though, and she learned by watching and listening, then she taught me what she had learned and how she had learned it. "Oh, I see," she'd say. "You're bearing down on your Rs" or "you're dropping your Gs." By the time we were through, I had probably learned more from her about how to teach accents than she had from me about how to use them.

"I thought it went pretty durned good," I told George when I had returned to his office. "As far as I'm concerned, she sounds like a Texan now." A couple of days later, I read in the trade papers that he had hired Mercedes to play Luz. I felt like I had something to do with her getting the part, and that made me feel damn proud.

While I waited on my next assignment, I spent time fixing up my office. The studio sent a few things over to dress it up, like western pictures and steer horns. They even sent some things from Gary Cooper's old office. Now, how about that! I was in Alan Ladd's dressing room with Gary Cooper's hand-me-downs! I was in movie cowboy heaven.

They also brought another couch and a good-sized coffee table because I told them I might have a number of people in there for "classes" on talking Texan. The studio didn't care why I wanted that furniture, and I'm not sure why I felt I had to justify it. The truth was, I didn't have any idea what I was doing, so I resorted to my old standby: guts and BS.

After a few days with very little to do other than to try to wake myself to make sure I wasn't dreaming, I got a call from George summoning me to his office. "Okay," I thought, "time to really start earning my supper."

I hustled over, where we "howdied" and shook hands, then George got right to the point. I always thought that was kind of rude—getting right to the point, I mean. Back in Texas, we never got right to the point. In fact, I've had many a conversation where we never got to the point at all, and when it was over we both wondered why we had talked in the first place. On the other hand, I wasn't in Texas anymore, so I supposed I shouldn't hold it against George if he got right to the point. After all, he wasn't a Texan, so he didn't know any better.

"I've got a young girl coming from New York City," he said. "Her name's Carroll Baker, and she'll be here any minute. I want you to work with her."

George explained that he was going to test Carroll for the role of the young Luz Benedict II, the daughter of Rock's Bick and Elizabeth's Leslie and namesake of Rock's sister. In the movie, Luz II infuriates her father because of her relationship with newly made oil millionaire Jett Rink, who was a thorn in Bick's side from the get-go. It was a star-making part for a young actress and a real opportunity for Carroll. Up until then, she'd mostly had small roles in TV shows and one small part in a movie called *Easy to Love,* with Esther Williams and Van Johnson. Most recently, she had been on Broadway, where she also had a bit part. Her number-one claim to fame at the time may have been being named Miss Florida Fruits and Vegetables of 1949. That would all change if she got this part in *Giant,* which would be her first major role.

George gave me the scene where Jett proposes to Luz II in a restaurant, and he wanted me to work on it with Carroll.

When she arrived a few minutes later, wearing jeans and with her blouse tied in a knot at her waist, she looked like a teenager, even though she was in her twenties. George introduced us, then said, "Bob is a real live Texan, and I've hired him to turn the whole cast into walking, talking Texans. I want you to go to his office with him and work on this scene. When we run the test, I want you to be as Texan as he is."

Not too much pressure, I don't suppose. I wonder, in hindsight, if this wasn't as much a test for me as it was for Carroll. After all, if I could turn Miss Florida Fruits and Vegetables into a Texan, I could turn anyone into a Texan.

We went back to my office and started to work. Carroll had gone to the Actor's Studio in New York and knew plenty about acting, but this was completely different from anything she had learned there. Still, she knew *how* to learn. Or, as we say in Texas, she was coachable. I spent a lot of time with her, sometimes just shooting the breeze, because she liked to hang out at my office and listen. As Mercedes did, Carroll picked up a lot by observing—watching how I moved and walked and memorizing how I talked, picking up the drawl and the cadence of my pronunciation. After a while, she was really getting the hang of it, and she almost had me convinced she had come from the flat plains of west Texas. I knew she'd do the same for George.

On the day of the screen test, I went with Carroll to lend moral support. After all, this was my test, too, and I wanted to see if my first pupil would pass. For some odd reason, George had brought in Tab Hunter to read James Dean's part opposite Carroll, even though Dean was likely available since he was filming another movie at the same studio. I say "for some odd reason" not out of any disrespect to Tab, who was a fine actor, but because I didn't see him as a Texan. He was too pretty. Not that a Texas man can't be "pretty," but no self-respecting cowboy would ever admit to it.

I saw right away when they started the test that not only was Tab too pretty, but he also had no idea of how to play a

Texan. He tried out a southern accent, like a lot of actors do—
even to this day—when they play Texans. They forget, or
maybe they never knew, that we Texans consider Texas the
West, not the South. That southern cornpone accent coming
out of a grown man's mouth sounds a little girly to me. Did
then and still does today.

Carroll, on the other hand, knew how to handle herself
like a real Texan. I could tell, though, that she was a little dis-
tracted at first by Tab's accent. She must have wondered if a
tornado had scooped up the Reata Ranch and moved it to
Mississippi. But then she got into a groove, and pretty soon I
plumb forgot about Tab Hunter. She had a drink, and she
kept playing with the straw and batting her eyes—I mean, she
just flat stole the scene. I knew then that she was going to do
all right because she had the equipment and the tempera-
ment and everything else she needed for the job.* George
hired her on the spot, and Luz Benedict II was ready to go.

No star was rising as fast or was on as steep a trajectory in 1955
as James Dean's. After a few minor roles and bit parts in television and the movies, this Indiana farm boy, who had also
honed his craft at the Actor's Studio in New York, exploded
into the big time playing Cal Trask in Elia Kazan's *East of Eden*.
That would lead to his first posthumous Academy Award nomination, which was also a first for Hollywood, for best actor in
a leading role. His second posthumous award would come
from *Giant*. Almost as quickly as his star rose, it flamed out
and crashed to earth on a lonely California highway near Pasa

---

*History bore out my prediction that Carroll would become a star if she
got the role. She would be nominated in 1957 for an Oscar for best actress in a leading role for playing the part of Baby Doll Meighan in *Baby
Doll*, scripted by Tennessee Williams and directed by Elia Kazan. That
same year she would win a Golden Globe for most promising newcomer,
sharing the award with Natalie Wood and Jayne Mansfield.

Robles. When you look back at the only three films in which he played major roles, the third being *Rebel Without a Cause*, the words of John Greenleaf Whittier leap to mind: "Of all the words of tongue or pen, the saddest are these: it might have been."

And oh, what might have been!

Since I had been on the job, I'd been eating lunch in the Green Room at the Warner Brothers commissary, trying to blend in with the stars and studio executives. The Green Room was essentially a private section for folks who didn't want to be bothered by gawkers and autograph hounds. Unlike the rest of the commissary, it had tablecloths and real silverware plus waiters and waitresses to take orders, and you didn't have to stand in a cafeteria line. The studio set it up as a tease because, even though it was a separate room, it was open to view for tourists. They could see the stars eating there, but they couldn't get close. Now that I think about it, it was kinda cruel.

I'll tell you, though, it was pretty heady stuff to be eating in the Green Room at Warner Brothers Studio. Anytime one of my friends came by for lunch, we'd eat there, and that's where I'd go with Sandy when she dropped by. Sometimes I'd eat with some of the cast of *Giant* or with some of my buddies, like Chill, who was in *Giant* but whom I knew before, or with Dub Taylor. I first met Dub when he came through Brownfield in 1945 and put on a quick-draw show before the Saturday morning movie at the local theater. He got his start in B westerns under the name Cannonball Taylor, but he was now branching out under the more dignified "Dub."

If any tourists saw me, they might have thought I was really somebody, but I doubt if I fooled anyone who *was* anyone. I had come to Hollywood intent on being the next John Wayne, but once I got there I realized Hollywood already had a John Wayne—and he did John Wayne pretty damn good! So

I had to settle, at least for now, for being a dialogue coach. Or maybe that was accent coach.

I first noticed Jimmy Dean, who was filming *Rebel Without a Cause* at Warner Brothers, in the Green Room. I was having lunch with Chill, who pointed him out and said, "Buckle, that's James Dean right over there." Chill always called me Buckle because of the rodeo trophy belt buckle I used to wear.

I figured people would be flocking around Jimmy after his recent star turn in *East of Eden* but, surprisingly, he was tucked off in a corner, head down, by himself at a table for two. He wore those big ol' horn-rimmed glasses like the smart kids in school used to wear. Us country boys, we'd go blind before we'd ever wear glasses, especially glasses like that.

I started watching for him after that, and he was always by himself. He smoked a lot, and as soon as he'd take his last bite, he'd light up a cigarette. When he'd leave, he'd keep his head down, as if watching the ground to see where he was stepping. One time he made eye contact with me, and I looked back at my plate kinda fast. I didn't want him to think I was staring at him, though I suspect he got a lot of that. Maybe the newness of his fame still hadn't worn off, or maybe boys from the Midwest farms simply were unaccustomed to the limelight, but for whatever reason, Jimmy rarely talked to or even acknowledged anyone while he ate.

Later, after he and I became friends, we ate together in the Green Room a lot. Once, after we'd had lunch and were walking back to my office, a reporter stopped us and asked Jimmy if he would do an interview. Jimmy said, "Hell no. You're not going to write what I tell you. You're going to write whatever you want to, so why don't you just go ahead and write it?" And he kept on walking.

The reporter shrugged his shoulders, as if he couldn't understand what had just happened. Nowadays it's not uncommon for movie stars to try to duck the paparazzi, but back in those days *no one* turned down interviews or dodged cameras.

It was all about getting publicity for yourself or your next movie. But Jimmy was different. He didn't give a damn about reporters. Still, there was something about him that got your attention, and you knew that he was special. What you couldn't know was how little time he had left on this earth. The Eagles said it best in their song "James Dean": "You were too fast to live, too young to die, bye-bye."

I was in my office one Friday afternoon, teaching the furniture to talk like Texans (you know, the strong silent types), when I heard a solid knock at the door. George hadn't given me any new assignments, so I wasn't expecting anybody. Anxious for human company, I couldn't get to the door fast enough. There stood Jimmy, dressed in his *Rebel* attire: jeans and a T-shirt. I figured I'd meet him sooner or later unless he pulled out of the part of Jett Rink, but I didn't expect him to come over unannounced.

"I'm Jimmy Dean," he said, as if I didn't know. "I've seen you at the commissary a few times. Can I come in and talk?"

"Sure, come on in." What else did he expect me to say? I'd have been disappointed if he hadn't wanted to come in.

Once inside, he looked around a bit, most likely amused at the western decor. "I understand that you've been hired to teach Rock Hudson to talk like a Texan."

"Yes sir, I have."

"I want you to help me create the character of Jett Rink. When I get into a part, I like to stay in that part and never come out of it until the picture's over. I want to be a Texan, twenty-four hours a day."

I had heard that about him. I also saw that as a bit of a problem. Right then he was filming *Rebel Without a Cause*, playing Jim Stark, a Los Angeles juvenile delinquent. I wasn't sure if there was room for both Jim Stark and Jett Rink in Jimmy's head at the same time. But what the hell, that's why I was getting paid the big bucks.

"That's the way to do it," I said. "If you're gonna be a Texan all day long, you gotta get up in the morning and put on your boots and hat. Dress like a Texan, eat the food Texans eat. The whole nine yards."

"That's what I want you to show me. I'll pay you out of my pocket."

"No need to do that. Warner Brothers is paying me pretty good. I'll be glad to work with you. When do you want to get started?"

"How about we go to dinner tonight after I get through on the *Rebel* set?"

Jimmy didn't have a car, having blown an engine in his Porsche Speedster in a race in Palm Springs, so he had only a motorcycle for transportation while the car was in the shop. At around six in the evening, I drove both of us to Barney's Beanery, damn near a tradition on Santa Monica Boulevard in West Hollywood. Over the years, Barney's had served the likes of Clark Gable, Errol Flynn, and Hoot Gibson. Now it would serve the likes of Robert Hinkle and James Dean.

The owner of Barney's, fortuitously named Barney, had hung a sign in bold letters over the bar: FAGGOTS—STAY OUT. It was not particularly friendly, certainly not acceptable in today's world, but not unheard of for that time.

Jimmy pointed to the sign and said, "That's why I like to come here."

A curious thing to say, I thought, but I didn't press it. It would be several months before Jimmy would open up to me and explain what he meant by that remark.

We found a table in a quiet corner—quiet being a relative term—and talked over hamburgers. I wasn't much of a drinker, so I had iced tea, and Jimmy had a soft drink. He was a little shy at first, feeling me out to see what kind of guy I was. Once he figured out that I was easy-going and that I didn't have an agenda to use him, he loosened up pretty quick. I expected him to be moody or brooding or a little oversold on himself, but he wasn't. He had a good sense of humor and liked to joke around. Even though he was the hottest thing in Hollywood, he acted like he was a new kid in the picture business and not a star. He was excited to be doing *Giant* and excited about *Rebel,* and his excitement showed. I liked him right up front.

Most of our conversation was about me, believe it or not. Jimmy wanted to know all about me—where was I from, how did I start rodeoing, how did I get into the picture business, was I married, and did I have a family? It's ironic that here I was with this big star, and it seemed like he was more interested in me than most folks would have been in him. I'd counter and ask him questions about himself, but he always managed to steer the conversation back to me.

I wanted to pay for his supper—I figured Warner Brothers would reimburse me—but he insisted on paying. After we settled up with Barney's, I drove us back to Warner's, and we went to my office to talk a little more. He made himself at home, and we ended up talking long into the night. Pretty soon, I started wondering just how long he was going to stay. I hoped my impatience didn't show, but I had a wife and two kids, including a new baby, waiting at home. Still, Jimmy kept talking. It seemed like he had a million questions about Texas. He wanted to know the differences in the regions of the state, and I explained how folks from different parts of the state had different accents, and you could tell where a person was from by the way he or she talked. He wanted to know where Marfa was, where we'd be shooting, and what he could expect when we got there.

I did find out that he was from Fairmount, Indiana, about sixty-five miles north of Indianapolis. He also told me that he was a Quaker. I didn't know what the hell a Quaker was other than seeing them in the movies with those funny-looking hats, but Jimmy didn't act like a movie Quaker; he acted like he was just one of us. And we had some things in common. I had played football in high school, and Jimmy was also an athlete, having played basketball. He said they called him "Rack," as in "Rack 'em up, Dean," because he was a pretty good shot from the outside. He got a little emotional when he talked about his mother dying when he was nine, and he said he didn't get along with his stepmother very well. His father had moved to Santa Monica, so he was close by, but Jimmy didn't visit him much because of his stepmother.

Jimmy's well of questions finally tapped out. Before he left, he gave me his phone number and said, "I need to get some western stuff to wear. Will you go with me?"

Professor Higgins not only had to teach Eliza Doolittle, the Cockney flower girl from George Bernard Shaw's *Pygmalion*, how to talk with a high-class accent, he also had to teach her how to dress and behave as though she came from high society. My role was no different. My backdrop, though, was Texas, not high-society England, and my tools would be boots, jeans, and cowboy hats. So we made an appointment to meet the next morning at a place on Van Nuys Boulevard called King's Western Wear. Then we said good-bye and went our separate ways.

When I got home, it was time to brag a bit. "Well, I met James Dean today."

That got Sandy's attention.

"He's a pretty good ol' boy," I said. "I'll bring him over some night so you can meet him. Maybe you can cook us some chicken fried steak."

I had told Jimmy that chicken fried steak was a prime example of what we would call "Texas eatin'." "Number one is barbecue," I'd told him. "And then comes chicken fried steaks and fried chicken."

I did invite Jimmy over a few days later, and Sandy cooked chicken fried steak, mashed potatoes and gravy, corn on the cob, and hot biscuits. If you're going to make a Texan out of a fella, you've got to make him *all* Texan. Jimmy really enjoyed that; you could tell just by watching him eat.

Sandy and I had two little boys—Mike, who was two, and Brad, who was just a few months old. Jimmy got right down on the floor and played with them. It didn't take long to seal our friendship, and we became lifelong friends—a short life for Jimmy, a long one for me, but I still consider him one of my best friends. And I still miss him.

But back to my mission to turn Jimmy into a Texan. I got to King's a little early the morning after our dinner at Barney's and went in to talk to Mr. King. I'd bought clothes from him before, so we knew each other.

"I'm bringing James Dean in here to buy some western stuff," I said.

"Who's James Dean?"

If I'd told him I was bringing in Rock Hudson, Mr. King would have known who that was, but he hadn't seen *East of Eden* and wasn't up on the latest Hollywood gossip. One of the girls who worked there knew who James Dean was, though, so Mr. King assigned her to wait on us. I'm telling you, you've never seen a more excited sales clerk when Jimmy came in and I introduced him. Nobody else in the store paid much attention to us because Jimmy didn't look and act like a movie star, and most folks didn't recognize him with those glasses on.

We lingered by the jeans section and looked them over. Back then, there weren't many choices—Lee's and Levi's—and they didn't come in numbers, like 501s and so forth. And styles? Loose fit, regular fit, boot cut, low ride, and so on? Forget it. Back then, your only choices were brand and size.

The clerk had been sizing him up mentally, just as I had. Jimmy wasn't very big. In fact, he was a little willowy, but I knew the cameras would make him look bigger. "What size?" she asked.

"Thirty-two thirty," he said.

"Nope," I said. "Give him thirty-two thirty-threes."

"What are you talking about?" he asked. "My size is thirty-two thirty."

"That may be the rebel without a cause's size, but that's not Jett Rink's size. When cowboys are out riding their horses, they don't want their pant legs riding up on their boots, so they always wear 'em long."

He shook his head, but he went along with me. After all, I was the expert. He ended up buying three pairs of jeans, three or four shirts, a pair of boots, a belt, and a straw cowboy hat.

When we got outside, I started taking the tags off the jeans. "Is there a laundry or a dry cleaner around here?" I asked.

"They're already clean."

"Clean's got nothing to do with it. Cowboys wear creases in their jeans, so we've got to get these laundried and starched. That takes the stiffness out of the material, then we put a crease in them. That's how real cowboys wear 'em."

There was that headshake again, but he went along with me once more. I suppose after the questions I had answered the night before, I had his confidence on all things Texas. We found a laundry and gave them instructions, then I took his hat and told him I'd pick up his clothes for him on Monday.

On Monday afternoon, Jimmy stopped by my office for his new duds. I waited while he tried on the jeans and boots, then I took his hat to the sink and stuck it under running water.

"What in the hell are you doing?" he asked. He had a shocked look on his face. Who could blame him? He thought I was ruining his brand-new hat that he had paid good money for.

"It softens the straw up so I can crease it and make it look like a real cowboy's hat."

Another shake of the head. He was probably wondering how much of this Texas nonsense he was going to have to put up with and if it was too late to pull out of the movie. When the hat was ready, I gave it to him and he put it on the back of his head. I stopped him real quick.

"Cowboys wear hats to keep the sun out of their faces. That means you've got to pull it down in front. If you're looking straight ahead and the brim of your hat's in view, you've got it on just about the right spot on your forehead."

And some folks think the hat is just a fashion statement. Ha!

He had bought a pair of Justin boots, and those needed some work, too. I'm telling you, as hard as it is to talk and act like a Texan, sometimes it's just as hard to dress like a Texan. I took each boot, one at a time, and bent the toe up until it damn near touched the top, then kept working it back and forth. Again, I had to explain what I was doing. Jimmy was real curious about things like that. He not only wanted to know what I was doing, he wanted to know *why* I was doing it. I explained that I was breaking the boots in so they wouldn't slip on his heels as he walked. I also told him he needed to wear the clothes a lot before we got to Texas so they'd look broken in and natural. He decided that he'd start by wearing them home, but he was afraid his hat would blow off when he rode his motorcycle, so he left it in my office.

The next day, still in his cowboy attire, he showed up to get his hat. I had gotten him some Bull Durham tobacco in a pouch and added that as an accessory by tucking it in his pocket with the tag hanging out. Then he wore it all to the set of *Rebel.* I imagine everybody must have done a double-take when he showed up looking like a twenty-four-year-old cowboy from west Texas. Somewhere, surely someone must have been singing the words to "Streets of Laredo": "I see by your outfit that you are a cowboy."

He took to wearing the cowboy getup to the *Rebel* set every day. After about a week Nick Ray, *Rebel*'s director, came to my office. Nick had directed John Wayne in *Flying Leathernecks* and had also been the director of *Johnny Guitar*.

"I understand you've been working with Jimmy on *Giant*," he said.

"Yeah, I have. If I do say so myself, I'm doing a good job of it."

He hesitated, then said, "I wish you'd ease up a bit. Jett Rink is starting to wear off a little on Jim Stark. Here I've got this guy who's supposed to be a big-city juvenile delinquent and he sounds more like John Wayne."

We had a good laugh over that. I assured Nick that I would get Jimmy to tone it down a bit, but I felt proud of my prize pupil.

I was happier than a gopher in soft dirt.

CHAPTER FIVE

Oh, Give Me a Home

We really stole Texas, didn't we, Mr. Benedict? I mean away
from Mexico?

—LESLIE LYNNTON

You're catching me a bit early to start joking, Miss Leslie.

—BICK BENEDICT

This was a very exciting time for Sandy and me. I would be
drawing a steady paycheck for about the next eight
months, and that would help us pay for the new house we had
just bought in North Hollywood, not far from Universal Studios. Even more than that, I knew this was an opportunity that
could open doors for me to advance my career.

As the time for actual production drew near, the cast for
Giant was set, and I was busy creating Texans from whole
cloth. On one of my visits to Jimmy on the *Rebel* set, he introduced me to nineteen-year-old Dennis Hopper, who was going
to play Jordy, Bick and Leslie's son in *Giant*. Dennis was fresh
in the business, just out of high school and raring to go. He
seemed to have a lot of sense for a young kid, very levelheaded
and determined to make his mark. He would let drugs get
him off track in the '60s and '70s, though, and I hated to see
that when it happened.

Following the success of *Easy Rider* in 1969, Dennis had a new
project he was going to write, direct, and star in for Universal

called *The Last Movie.* It nearly ended up being the last movie, all right—for Dennis Hopper. Dennis called Chill and offered him a part in the picture, which was about a western being made in Peru that goes very wrong. Though it was actually to be filmed in Peru, it was sort of an inside story about Hollywood and the making of movies that, arguably, was about its own making.

"You got a part for Buckle?" Chill asked.

"Sure. Bring him along."

Good ol' Chill, always looking out for me.

My part in that picture lasted just long enough for Chill's agent to find out he had agreed to do the film with Dennis. "No!" he said. "You get down there in South America with Dennis and all those drugs, and you'll have a mess on your hands. You don't want to have anything to do with that."

With Chill out, I was out, too, but in a stroke of luck, losing that job turned out to be one of the best things that ever happened to me. It's a shame Dennis didn't lose that job, too. According to *The Village Voice, The Last Movie* was one of the "druggiest" movies ever made—putting it in a likely dead heat with *Easy Rider*—and one that nearly "incinerated" his career. In his book *Easy Riders, Raging Bulls* (Simon and Schuster 1998), Peter Biskind called it a "devastating personal defeat" for Dennis. It could have been for me, too, if I'd gotten involved in it.

But in 1955, things hadn't taken that downturn for Dennis. He really wanted to be a good actor, and that meant he really wanted to be a Texan in *Giant*, so he asked me to work with him. He always had a big smile on his face and was very grateful for my help. I enjoyed seeing his career develop.

Pretty soon, Jimmy, Carroll, Dennis, and I were hanging out together, just like a bunch of high school kids. Sometimes others from the *Rebel* set joined us, including Natalie Wood. Even though she was only seventeen at the time, Natalie had already been acting for more than a decade. Our paths would cross again in the future.

George Stevens found other jobs for me as we started to gear up. "Don't bring any wardrobe for me to look at," George told the wardrobe department, "unless Bob Hinkle has approved it." That didn't set too well with the wardrobe guy. After all, that was his job and here I was, some interloper, being given veto authority over how he did it. He came to my office in a snit: "Just what the hell do you know about wardrobe?"

"I don't know very much," I said, "but I reckon we better do what Mr. Stevens says." Pretty good advice, I thought. He thought so, too, and it calmed him down. I didn't want to tick him off, but I did want to do *my* job. The last thing we wanted was for the cast to show up in hokey drugstore cowboy outfits that real Texans wouldn't wear even if they had to go naked instead. Still, I had to walk a fine line of diplomacy.

Just when I thought I had that little hiccup smoothed over, I ran into the same problem with the casting folks over the minor cast and extras. George gave them the same instructions he had given wardrobe, essentially vesting me with final approval over their choices. But if George wanted it, George got it, and that was my saving grace.

Watching George Stevens work on *Giant* was a real education, not just in the ways of directing but also in psychology. George was a master psychologist. I thought directing was about telling people to do what you wanted them to do. What I learned from George was that directing is really about *allowing* people to do what you want them to do by making them think it was their idea. Make sense? Well, let me show you what I'm talking about.

One of the first things we shot was an interior scene that, in the movie, takes place in Virginia, where the story starts. We filmed it on a soundstage at Warner Brothers that doubled as the dining room of the Lynnton house. This is where Leslie Lynnton, Elizabeth's character, first meets Bick, who tries to impress her with his prowess as a Texas rancher and landowner. Leslie stays up all night studying about Texas. The next morning at breakfast, instead of being impressed, she puts Bick on the defensive: "We really stole Texas, didn't we, Mr. Benedict? I mean away from Mexico."

She quickly learns that Texans don't take kindly to those kinds of things. "You're catching me a bit early to start joking, Miss Leslie," Bick says.

The conversation spirals downward from there. "I've never heard anything as ignorant as some eastern people," Bick says. "You all think that the glory happened here in the East, don't you, with Valley Forge and Bunker Hill? Do you know about San Jacinto? Have you heard about the Alamo?" By the time Leslie's mother enters the scene, the two young people can barely look at each other. Ultimately, they do get married, but that's no sure thing in this scene.

George had them rehearse a few times, but Rock and Liz weren't getting what he wanted. Rock overacted a bit, almost as if he were in a silent movie—using broad gestures and facial expressions, practically mugging for the camera. Liz, for her part, was a little too flighty when she poked at Rock. The tone just wasn't right. Finally, George turned to me and said, loud enough for everyone to hear, "Bob, get your script and come to my office." Then he called to his assistant director and told him to bring Liz and Rock as well.

George's office was in one of the dressing room bungalows on the soundstage, with a desk, chairs, and couch set up near a small bed. Liz, Rock, and I gathered and waited for our instructions. "Bob," he said, "I want you to read Rock's lines, and Rock, you just listen. I don't want you to do it like Bob, but I just want you to listen. Liz, I want you to do Judith's part." Judith Evelyn was playing the role of Nancy Lynnton, Leslie's mother.

We were a little confused by the instructions. Why not have Liz read her own part instead of Judith's?

"Do you want me to read the lines like Judith does?" Liz asked.

"Don't act, just read the lines. And I'm going to read your lines."

Well, that was about as clear as mud, with a man reading a young woman's part and a young woman reading an older woman's part. But we figured George was going to change some dialogue, so we thought we'd humor him. After all, he was the director.

We went through the scene once, just a cold, dry reading of the lines. George wasn't a much better actor than I was, and his reading of Liz's lines didn't sound any better than my reading of Rock's. Liz reading Judith's wasn't all that bad, though, if you overlooked the obvious age reversal. If this had been for real, the scene would have made the cutting room floor in a hurry.

After we finished, we waited to see what changes George wanted to make.

"Okay, let's do it again."

As little sense as it made to do it once, doing it twice made half as much. But like I said, he was the director, so we did it again.

"One more time," George said.

Mount Elizabeth Taylor erupted. "Damn it, George, what the f—— do you want me to do? I don't understand what you're trying to do here."

Cowboys hear a lot of cussing. Nothing new about that, and I'd heard more than my share hanging around rodeos. But this was the first time I'd ever heard a woman use that word. And not just any woman, either. It was Elizabeth Taylor—*National Velvet* Elizabeth Taylor, *Little Women* Elizabeth Taylor, *A Place in the Sun* (where she'd worked with George before) Elizabeth Taylor—using the F word. As shocking as that was, what was even more shocking was that Rock didn't pay any attention to it, and neither did George. Apparently, it was old hat to them.

"All I want you to do is read the line," George said patiently, like a daddy talking to a wayward child. So we went through it one more time, then George said, "Okay, let's go shoot it."

That was it. Didn't tell them a thing about what they should or shouldn't do or how they should or shouldn't read the lines. Just "let's go shoot it."

I hadn't been in the picture business all that long, and I'd never been that close to a director, and I damn sure hadn't worked that close to major stars like this before. I didn't know if this was the way they usually handled things, but it seemed to me a word or two of explanation from George might have been in order. I mean, aren't directors supposed to . . . well, direct?

We went back to the set and shot the scene without any more rehearsing. "That's great," George said. "Perfect." Then he went on to the next scene. Pretty soon, the whole thing was forgotten—at least it seemed that way—by everybody but me. I was still trying to figure out just what in the hell was going on. What kind of nuts had I gotten myself involved with?

The next day, when George was ready to look at the rushes, he asked Liz, Rock, and me to sit with him. "Rushes" are the overnight "rush" development of what was filmed the day before, so the director can see what worked, what didn't, and what needed to be re-shot. There was a little console where George sat and handled the controls. He typically sat there by himself, but this time he wanted Rock and Liz on either side of him.

George hit the switch to dim the lights, then started the projector. As we watched the scene unfold, we saw that George had been right—it was perfect. Bick Benedict was royally PO'd at Leslie Lynnton, with tension in his face and curt answers to her questions, because Rock Hudson was royally PO'd at George Stevens; and Leslie Lynnton was not nearly as flighty because George Stevens had taken the edge off of Elizabeth Taylor.

When George stopped the projector, he asked, "Do you see what I was trying to do?"

Oh yeah, we got it. Everybody got it. Rock later told me, "I'm never gonna question that man again."

On May 30 we flew a chartered airplane to Charlottesville, Virginia, to film the exterior scenes at the Lynnton home. I remember the date because it was Memorial Day, and we flew directly over the Indianapolis Motor Speedway while the Indy 500 was in progress. If you looked out the window on my side of the plane, you could see the track. The pilot came over the public address system to give us an update on the race, then he said, "Wait a minute, there's been an accident."

We later found out that a driver named Bill Vukovich, who had won the race in both 1953 and 1954, had been killed in an accident while leading the pack on the fifty-seventh lap. A car Vukovich was lapping swerved because of a broken axle, then hit another car about to be lapped and knocked it directly into Vukovich's path. The collision sent Vukovich's car airborne, and it landed upside down on the other side of the retaining wall. Looking back on it now and knowing what later happened to Jimmy at Pasa Robles, I wonder if it had been an omen.

We were only in Virginia for about a week, but that was long enough for me to get my first on-screen role in a big Hollywood movie, brief and unrecognizable though it was. One of the little-known actors in *Giant*, who had also appeared in *Black Beauty*, was Fury, a splendid-looking horse trained by Ralph McCutcheons. Fury's registered name was Highland Dale; I guess even the animals in Hollywood had stage names. In the movie, Bick has heard about this magnificent horse

Rock Hudson and Bob, on the set of *Giant* in Virginia (June 1955). Bob dressed like Hudson so he could double him on horseback. Courtesy of Bob Hinkle.

named Warwinds and wants to buy him for his bloodline, to stud with his mares. So he goes to Virginia from his ranch in Texas to check out the horse at the Lynnton estate. That's when he first sees Leslie, riding Warwinds in a foxhunt.

Fury was a very spirited horse, which made for great visuals on-screen when Bick rode him—doing spins, backing him up, and doing figure eights. What it also meant, though, was that it took a better horseman than Rock Hudson to do the things they needed to have done. Nothing against Rock, who was a better actor than I'll ever dream of being, but yours truly knew a bit more about riding spirited horses than Rock did. Most of my work ended up on the cutting room floor, but if you look real close—and real fast—the next time you watch *Giant*, you'll see the back of a west Texas cowboy taking that horse through his paces.

The next stop after Virginia was Marfa, Texas, the county seat of Presidio County. Marfa was a town of a couple thousand people slap-dab in the middle of the Big Empty, between the Davis Mountains and Big Bend National Park. Or, as some would say, midway between nothing and nowhere.

Why Marfa? Well, this part of the state made sense if you were looking for a place to make a movie about a ranch of over a half-million acres because there's miles and miles of miles and miles. As I understand it, while George was scouting the Big Bend area, he came across the Worth Evans Ranch, about fifteen miles west of Marfa on Highway 90 that goes from San Antonio to El Paso, and the location was set.

At the time, Marfa was best known (if it was known at all) for the "Marfa Lights" that mysteriously appear flickering on the horizon out toward the Chinanti Mountains, dancing and diving, moving around, then suddenly disappearing. The first record of them that I'm aware of is a report from a young cowhand driving cattle through the Paisano Pass in 1883. I've seen them myself, though to me they look like the headlights of a vehicle on the way to Mexico. But who am I to bust myths? And there were certainly no cars out there in 1883.

In more recent times, Marfa has become somewhat of a tourist destination, an artsy town known for its architecture, modern art, and the nearby Big Bend. Since *Giant* showed the world the wonders of Marfa, other film crews have discovered it as well, including those of *There Will Be Blood* and *No Country for Old Men*. Both of those movies made characters out of the west Texas landscape as surely as *Giant* did. And even though none of it was filmed in Marfa, the 1981 play *Come Back to the Five and Dime, Jimmy Dean, Jimmy Dean*, which was turned into a movie the next year by Robert Altman, was set in Marfa. Both the play and the movie starred Cher and marked her "coming out" as a serious actress after years of trying.

We flew into Marfa on one of those big TWA twin tails and landed at an old airbase that had been built during the war for bombers to use for doing training runs. The members of the cast who had not gone to Virginia had arrived in Marfa the day before, and they met us at the airstrip. Among them were Chill, Monte Hale, Jane Withers, Carroll Baker, Dennis Hopper, and Jimmy.

The studio had rented houses for some of the cast, while the rest of us bunked at the historic Paisano Hotel. Chill, Jimmy, and Rock shared a house in town. Jane Withers stayed in a house by herself, and Liz shared one with her hairdresser, Patricia Westmore. Liz and Patricia converted the third bedroom of their house into a beauty shop for a clientele of one.

I shared a room at the Paisano with Monte Hale, which was a bit of a problem. He and I were both over six feet tall, and all we had to sleep on were two little ol' half-size (or so it seemed) beds. When we lay down, our feet hung completely over the ends of the beds. Yeah, boy, the life of a Hollywood star is certainly glamorous.

Monte was yet another Texas connection on the picture. He was born in San Angelo, about three hundred miles east of Marfa, and grew up picking guitars and performing in places like Galveston and Houston before breaking into B westerns as a singing cowboy. I first met Monte in 1947, two years after I met Dub Taylor, when he, too, paid a visit to Brownfield. I knew Monte and I were going to get along just fine—and we did for the past half-century.

After all the howdies and hugs at the airport, Jimmy took me aside and asked, "Bob, do you think we could go rabbit hunting tonight?"

I guess I had whetted his appetite because I kept telling him that once we got to Texas I'd take him hunting. He bought a rifle in Hollywood, a lever action like those old model 94 30–30s they use in the movies, and brought it with him based on my promises. I didn't have a gun, so I borrowed a .22 from the manager at the hotel, and we set out in the car Warner's had rented for Jimmy.

Our first stop was Livingston Hardware to buy shells. Livingston was near the hotel, and it sold a bit of everything, from hardware to clothes—mostly western stuff, like boots and hats—to hunting supplies. During the time we were filming in Marfa, Jimmy and I became regular customers of the store and got to know its owner, Jimmy Livingston, real well. Prices were reasonable, especially by Hollywood standards. We could buy a carton of shells for five dollars, which translated into a penny a shell, so we bought a bunch of hollow points for long rifles, then it was off to the hunt.

Before you get all riled up about us shooting rabbits, I gotta tell you that these weren't those cute little cottontails like kids get for pets. These were west Texas jackrabbits, big ol' things with long ears and fast enough to outrun a horse. They were more of a nuisance than anything, considered by ranchers to be as big a pest as coyotes. Keep in mind that this was arid west Texas, where brown was the color of the day, the year, and the millennium. To top it off, this part of the state was smack in the middle of a drought, which made folks long for the arid days of yore. It was so dry the cowboys were spitting cotton and the trees were bribing dogs. The grass was either brown or nonexistent, and that meant the cattle had to scrounge for every blade.

Now, throw a bunch of rabbits into the mix with this little-known fact: Texas lore has it that three jackrabbits could eat as much grass as a cow. That may be another Texas tall tale, but the fact is they were more than just a nuisance; they were a downright threat to cattle. A bounty of a nickel an ear had been placed on them, and at some point the ranchers got together and poisoned a bunch to preserve grazing for their starving cattle. So it's not like Jimmy and I were shooting cats and dogs. No sir, we were doing a public service for the ranchers of west Texas.

When we hunted, we didn't have to go into any pastures or fields. All we had to do was drive up and down those old country roads at night, and on both sides we'd find all the jackrabbits we wanted. They liked to come close to the pavement for some reason. When we spotted one, we'd ease to the side of the road. I'd whistle to get the rabbit's attention, and he'd usually stop and raise his head, looking for the sound. That would give the shooter time to draw a bead and fire. Jimmy and I would take turns shooting. He got hooked on rabbit hunting. I mean, he really loved it.

One time, Jane Withers asked to go with us. Jane had recently married singer Kenneth Errair, of the Four Freshmen, and *Giant* was a comeback of sorts for this former child star, whose last movie had been in 1947. She's probably best known, though, for her role as Josephine the Plumber in the Comet cleanser television commercials in the 1960s and 1970s. Jane's rabbit hunting experience was not a pleasant one. We came across a coyote that had gotten caught and badly injured in a barbed wire fence. We couldn't just leave it there to suffer, and we weren't able to free it from the wire without exposing ourselves to injury (coyotes have wicked teeth), so I had no choice but to shoot it in the head to put it out of its misery. That nearly made Jane sick. After that, she had no interest in going rabbit hunting again.

But Jimmy and I were the great white hunters. Sometimes we'd kill thirty or forty rabbits in a hunt. We'd cut the ears off and put them in a tow sack, then leave the rest of the carcass for the coyotes or the buzzards. We'd take the ears to Livingston Hardware and trade them for .22 shells. Pretty soon, word about us got around, as we came in day after day with our tow sack full of ears. One local rancher made a deal with Jimmy Livingston: "When those boys come down here with their ears, tell them to hunt out at my place, and I'll furnish all the shells they want. Put it on my account."

We never had to buy shells again. After a while, Jimmy Livingston told us to stop bringing in the rabbit ears because we were overloading him. We had about two hundred ears in the tow sack in the back of Jimmy's car, but Livingston wouldn't take them. They were starting to get a little ripe, so I got to thinking about how to get rid of them, and an idea hit me.

"You know what, Jimmy? Ol' Jack Warner back there at Warner Brothers told me to get him a pair of boots."

"Yeah. So?"

"So here's what I'm going to do," I went on, as the plan took shape in my head. "I'm gonna run over there to the hardware store and get me an empty boot box." I could see the smile starting on Jimmy's face; he was way ahead of me. "Then I'm going to stuff it full of rabbit ears and send it to Jack."

By the time I got the words out, we were both bent over laughing. It seemed like a good idea at the time, but looking back on it now, maybe it wasn't my brightest idea. If I'd known then what I know now about Jack Warner, I damn sure wouldn't have done it.

I first met Jack Warner, the head of the studio, when he and his son-in-law, Bill Orr, were walking to the set they were building for *Giant*. Bill was the executive producer on two Warner Brothers television westerns, *Maverick* and *Cheyenne*, and I'd met him before at the commissary. Bill introduced me to Jack as the guy they had hired to teach Rock and Jimmy to be Texans. I didn't know that peons like me weren't supposed to hobnob with the executives, so I invited them both to my office, which was close by.

I can only imagine what Jack must have thought of my pitiful office, with its steer horns and guns hanging on the walls. I was mighty proud of it, but I'm sure it bore no resemblance to the executive side of the studio. I guess it wasn't too offputting, though, because after that, Jack would stop by from time to time just to shoot the bull. I'm sure some of that was because I was close to Jimmy, who was the hottest thing in Hollywood at the time, but it was also because I was starting to get some publicity in the trades, mostly for working with Jimmy. I guess Jack wanted to keep up with what was going on with his people.

One time he got off telling stories about his days in vaudeville. He did a little soft shoe, to show me he still had it, I guess. I remember thinking to myself, "Can you believe that? There's the head of Warner Brothers Studio dancing in my office." I never would have believed I'd be hanging out with the likes of Jack Warner. He could have made a big star out of me if he had wanted to, but he never once mentioned putting me in the movies. I wonder how differently my life would have turned out if he had.

Anyway, back to the rabbit ears and bad ideas. I was young then, and I wasn't about to let fear and common sense hold me back. Jimmy and I went to Livingston Hardware, and, sure enough, they gave us an empty boot box. We crammed it full of those rotten-smelling jackrabbit ears. Each ear was probably about eight inches long and two-and-a-half to three inches wide, and they fit good and solid. I wrote all the address you needed in those days: Jack Warner, Warner Brothers Studio, Burbank, California. No street address, no zip code. Like addressing something just to Santa Claus, North Pole. It'd get there.

A few days later Tom Andre, our production manager, drove out to the set. Tom didn't usually show up unless there was a problem, so he had our attention just by being there, especially with the look he was wearing on his face.

"George, I got a call from Jack Warner," he said. "I don't know how serious it is, but he's got a message for Bob and Jimmy."

George looked my way. "You know what this is about?"

"No," I lied.

"Where's Jimmy?"

"He's over yonder in his dressing room."

"Get him and come over here."

I did as I was told, and Jimmy and I came back like two little kids who'd been called on the carpet by the principal. Except it might be worse than that. George was the principal, but Jack was the superintendent of the whole school system. We stood there and waited for our punishment.

"We just got a message from Jack Warner back in Hollywood," George said. "You do know who Jack Warner is, don't you?"

"Yes sir," we said in unison.

"Jack Warner, Warner Brothers? Ring a bell?"

"Yes."

"Okay, I'm going to give you the message just like it was delivered to me." A dramatic pause. "Jack said, 'I'm going to kill those two SOBs personally—that Jimmy Dean and that Bob Hinkle.'"

He paused again, then said, "Now what in the hell is going on?"

It was all Jimmy and I could do to keep straight faces, but we knew we couldn't laugh. At least not yet. We didn't know if we were really in trouble, but George sure wasn't smiling.

The guilty dog usually barks first and loudest. I looked at Jimmy and said, "Well, I guess he got his boots."

Jimmy and I laughed so hard I thought we'd bust a gut. I finally calmed down enough to tell George what we'd done, then we had another good laugh that included George—much to our relief. Naturally, I hurried to Livingston's as soon as we reached town to get Jack some real boots. He wanted black, so I bought him a nice pair of 9Ds and sent them to Hollywood right away, to cool him down.

Later, when we returned to Hollywood, Warner Brothers threw a big welcome party, and Jack was there, showing off his boots to everybody. I asked, "Jack, didn't that first pair fit you?"

"I still ought to kill you," he said.

Then he told everybody the story, and they really got a kick out of it. Even Jack laughed. Through the laughter, Chill leaned over to me and said, "Buckle, you got more guts than an army mule to do something like that."

I found out later that Jack had a reputation for being difficult to deal with. One director said Jack was mean just for the sake of meanness. I heard a story about an actor under contract who had written Jack to express his pleasure at working for Warner Brothers, and Jack thought he was getting a little too familiar—so he had him fired. I suppose that was why George wasn't happy when he first got that message on the set. But Jack had always been friendly with me, so I thought I could be friendly with him right back, even pull a prank or two. I guess my story could have ended then and there. Fortunately, Jack was a good sport about it, which was no more a sure thing than Bick and Leslie's wedding after that first scene.

Call me lucky.

CHAPTER SIX

Howdy, Friends and Neighbors

Where the hell did that bullet go?

—Bob Hinkle

I don't know. I've heard sometimes that when you get shot,
you don't feel it at first. Like you're in shock or something.

—James Dean

What started as a job soon turned into the most fun I had ever had. When you're working with a group of strangers who turn out to be your friends, that has a funny way of happening. In addition to Jimmy, I became very close friends with Chill Wills while we were in Marfa. I never forgot that he's the one who first got me onto the studio lot at Universal and that he started a chain reaction that ended up with me now being on the set of *Giant* in Marfa.

Chill gave everyone he liked a nickname. As I already mentioned, mine was Buckle. He called Monte Hale "Montz," a name I call Monte to this day, and he called Jimmy "the Spook." Chill, who shared a house with Jimmy and Rock, said Jimmy would come into the kitchen every morning wearing just his underwear, boots, and cowboy hat to get juice out of the icebox. I came by early one morning to pick up Jimmy, and Chill turned to Rock and said, "Isn't that a sight? Double Buckle Cowboy and the Spook." And it just stuck.

In the lobby of the Paisano Hotel in Marfa, Texas, on Monte Hale's birthday (June 8, 1955). *Left to right:* Marcia Fuller, Jimmy Dean, unidentified man, Monte, and Bob. Courtesy of Bob Hinkle.

Sometimes in the evenings, we'd hang out in the lobby of the Paisano Hotel, and Monte would bring along his guitar and sing. Jimmy really enjoyed that, so I bought him a cheap guitar and, since I had been playing guitar for years, taught him how to play it. His favorite song was "Cattle Call," an Eddy Arnold song, and he made Monte do it over and over again until he learned it himself.

One weekend, Chill drove to Mexico and came back with a really nice guitar. He hid it behind Jimmy's usual chair, then he took Jimmy's old guitar and put it on the seat. As we gathered later for our sing-along, he walked over as if he had never seen the old one before.

"What the hell is this?" He grabbed the guitar by the neck and smashed it across the back of the chair.

Jimmy Dean, on the set of *Giant*, with two of the kids from the Mexican village on the Reata Ranch (June—July 1955). Photograph by Richard C. Miller. Courtesy of the Miller Family Trust A. © Miller Family Trust A. All rights reserved.

Jimmy hustled over and snatched the pieces out of Chill's hands. I could see that he was really PO'd. "What the hell did you do that for? That's my guitar."

"That piece of crap's not a guitar," Chill said. He took the new one from its hiding place behind the chair and handed it to Jimmy. "Now, this is a guitar."

Jimmy didn't know what to do. He felt bad for yelling at Chill and a bit embarrassed. So, very un-Texan like, he gave

Chill a sheepish hug, which was his way of saying "I'm sorry" and "thank you" at the same time.

I shouldn't have been surprised that Jimmy learned to play the guitar. He was one of the most competitive people I've ever known, and that includes some world champion cowboys I've been around over the years, such as Jim Shoulders, Casey Tibbs, and Larry Mahan. Jimmy didn't want to be second-best at anything, not even guitar playing. Anything you'd teach him, he'd practice like an obsession. Next thing you know, he was as good as or better than you. He seemed to take for granted that he'd master whatever he put his mind to. He used to joke that he would win an Oscar one day and for an acceptance speech he'd simply say "you're welcome," then sit down.

Monte was on the set one day playing with a short length of rope, about a quarter of an inch thick, with a small rock tied in a knot on the end. He would swing the rope around his head, then with what seemed like just a couple of twists and a flick of his wrist, he would throw a half-hitch around the end and sort of pop that knot through the half-hitch.

"How'd you do that?" I asked.

"Easy. You just—" Then he showed me again.

I caught on pretty fast because I had grown up working with ropes, especially at the rodeo. I even did a little trick roping for fun, butterflies and flat spins and other tricks. I showed Jimmy what I learned from Monte. Of course, he wanted to learn how to do it. Pretty soon he had the trick down, too. After that, I had the prop department bring over more ropes, and I expanded my "talk like a Texan" school with Jimmy to include trick roping. We set up a bale of hay on the set to lasso, and Jimmy and I would spend hours practicing. I taught him how to rope a calf, tying up one front foot and two back feet, and sometimes he'd practice on me. Since I only had two feet, he'd use one of my hands as the front foot.

Bob and George Stevens, Jr., at the 2006 premiere of the fiftieth-year
rerelease of the movie *Giant.* Stevens Jr. was on the set on occasion while
Giant was being filmed. Courtesy of Bob Hinkle.

Another time, I saw this rope hanging down about two
feet off of a microphone on the sound boom, with a knot at
the end known as a monkey's fist. I asked the soundman how
it got there, and he told me he had learned it in the navy. I
had him teach me, then I taught Jimmy. Before you knew it,
Jimmy had not only mastered all the tricks I knew, but he was
inventing new tricks of his own. We carried those ropes with
us everywhere, constantly working with them and even teaching our tricks to other people.

Jimmy wasn't perfect with the ropes, though. One time
later, when we were back in Hollywood, he came to the house
for dinner and got to horsing around with a knotted rope. He
swung it over his head a time or two. Too late, I saw Mike, my

Jimmy Dean on the set of *Giant* (1955). Courtesy of Bob Hinkle.

two-year-old, wander into the rope's flight path. Before either Jimmy or I could react—WHAP—that ol' knot bounced off his head. I think it scared Mike more than it hurt him, but he cried as if he'd been stuck with a pin.

Jimmy dropped the rope and grabbed Mike. "Oh, I'm sorry, Mike. I didn't mean to do that."

"It's all right," I said. "It was just an accident."

I felt as bad for Jimmy as I did for Mike. He couldn't stop apologizing—to Mike, to Sandy, to me. He really felt bad about it. For years after that, we'd sometimes ask Mike, "Who hit you in the head with a rope" and he'd say, "Jimmy Dean." So for all you parents who think kids don't remember the trauma of their youth, let that be a lesson to you.

Back to Texas, where I also taught Jimmy how to roll his own cigarettes. I didn't smoke, but I'd been around enough smokers to learn how to do it. He and I would roll up a few at the start of the day, then Jimmy put them in his shirt pocket to use in the scenes. I taught him how to saddle and unsaddle a horse, how to properly mount and dismount, and a lot of little things about riding. About the only thing he didn't master was chewing tobacco. When he tried, he would swallow a big mouthful of the juice before he could spit it out. It made him sick at his stomach, so he gave up on it pretty quick.

Jimmy's competitive streak nearly got me killed one time. We were heading back to town one evening after a full day of filming, and Jimmy was trucking along on empty Highway 90, going about sixty or seventy miles an hour. Jimmy liked to drive fast. He was into racing cars, so I knew you couldn't hold him back too long.

He glanced in the rearview mirror and said, "Here comes Clay."

Clay Evans, rancher Worth Evans's youngest son, was about nineteen years old and hung around on the set with Jimmy and me. I looked back and saw Clay's new car catching us. He got right on our tail, then pulled into the oncoming lane to pass. Just as he nosed ahead, Jimmy kicked it into overdrive. We inched ahead of Clay, who accelerated in front again. We went back and forth like that for a bit, running side by side on that two-lane highway, hollering and yelling at each other. Just as we went over a hill, I saw a car stopped in our lane. A woman stood on the side of the road, looking at her tires like she had a flat. Now it was a game of high-speed chicken, except we were going to lose to the stopped car.

"Let him pass," I said, hands braced on the dashboard.

Jimmy eased up on the gas, but Clay wasn't passing. I saw that he had eased up, too, to let us in front of him. They both realized their mistake at the same time. Jimmy floored it again—just as Clay did. By now, I could see the proverbial whites of that woman's eyes. We had reached the point of no return, and it wouldn't matter who slowed down or who sped up. I squeezed my eyes shut and braced harder against the dash.

Jimmy suddenly cut the wheel to the right. I felt us going airborne and opened my eyes. We shot off the road onto the hard west Texas dirt and zipped past that poor woman. Suddenly, our tires hit soft sand. The car swung sideways, with my door aimed straight for a big signpost. Before I could say a quick prayer, Jimmy threw the car into second, gunned it, fishtailed a bit, and we were back on the road alongside Clay again, as if we had never left pavement.

I don't know what happened to that woman, but I suspect whoever did her laundry learned exactly how scared she really was. Some of the film crew came along a few minutes later, not knowing what had happened. They saw all that dust still swirling and tire tracks leading off the road. They must have thought we had disintegrated because no wreckage was in sight.

I sometimes think that set the stage for what would later happen to Jimmy. If I believed in omens, that episode, like Bill Vukovich's crash at the Indy 500, would have been one.

It's a wonder Jimmy and I didn't kill each other long before his tragic accident. I remember another time when we barely dodged a bullet—literally. It happened on one of our rabbit hunts. It was my time to shoot, so I sat in the passenger seat and Jimmy drove, but he was trying to reload his gun at the same time. He moved along nice and slow, about fifteen miles an hour, with the butt of his gun toward me, the barrel pointed at the door. He pulled the lever back and tucked a bullet into the chamber, then just as he shut the lever—POW!

The sound about scared me out of my pants. Jimmy slammed on the brakes—if you can call it "slamming" at fifteen mph. I looked at him, his face white as death. "What the hell was that?" I asked.

"I think my gun went off."

I wanted to say, "You *think* your gun went off? Wouldn't you *know* if your gun went off in your lap?" But I didn't. Instead I asked, "Did it hit you?"

"I don't think so."

He ejected a shell from his rifle—sure enough, a spent shell. We got out of the car and checked the door. No hole in the cloth on the inside. No exit hole on the outside.

"Did you shoot out the window?" I asked. The window was rolled down, so that seemed like a possibility.

"The barrel wasn't aimed that high."

"Where the hell did that bullet go?" This was starting to get a little weird.

"I don't know. I've heard sometimes that when you get shot, you don't feel it at first. Like you're in shock or something."

I had to admit, he did look pale enough to be in shock. I grabbed his arm and dragged him in front of the car, into the high beams. "Lift your shirt up."

He did. I leaned in close and checked him over. No blood. Not even a graze mark.

"What about your legs?" I asked.

He dropped his britches and we checked his legs. Still no blood.

It's a good thing those old west Texas roads are deserted at night because if someone had come along, we'd have added

Jimmy Dean and Bob watching a cattle roundup on the Reata Ranch (June 1955). Courtesy of Bob Hinkle.

a whopper to the rumor mill, standing out there in the middle of nowhere and Jimmy with his pants down.

We finally decided, as improbable as it seemed, that he must have shot out the window, so we went on with our hunting. When it came time to head back to town, Jimmy grabbed the handle to roll up the window. As the glass rose from the inside of the door, we saw a perfect bullet hole right through the middle. The folds in the cloth on the inside of the door had covered the hole, which is why we couldn't see it in the dark. We learned later that there is a steel arm about an inch thick that moves the window up and down, and the bullet went through the glass and hit that, then ended up flattened inside the door. When word got out that we had to order another window because ours had a bullet hole in it, a rumor started that we had shot a rancher's cow and he had plugged a 30–30 through our car in retaliation. There was always some kind of rumor going around, so I guess we got off lucky. Like I said, if someone had come along and found Jimmy out there with his pants down . . .

The truth is, Jimmy and I were having the time of our lives. We were just a couple of twenty-four-year-old kids in the middle of west Texas, without parental authority around. We were always getting into some kind of mischief, like sending jackrabbit ears to Jack Warner or racing on country roads or shooting out car windows. We found a street sign in Marfa at the intersection of Texas and Dean streets, so we just had to steal it. Today, that sign is in the James Dean Museum in Fairmount, Indiana. I suppose if there'd been watermelon patches out there, we'd have been stealing watermelons, too.

One day at the end of filming, Jimmy and I were planning another round of rabbit hunting. Night fell pretty shortly after the end of our workday, so we usually got to our hunting location right about dark. "You want to go by the hotel first and see if you got any mail?" Jimmy asked.

Sandy wrote once or twice a week, and I had just gotten a letter from her a day or so earlier, so I figured there was nothing. "Nah, let's go on out there from here."

"It's still a little early, so we may as well go by the hotel first. Won't hurt to check."

I didn't think anything of it at the time, so we went to the hotel and, sure enough, I didn't have any mail. "But someone left a package for you," the desk clerk said. She handed me a long box. Inside was a beautiful, brand-new Remington pump rifle.

"Boy, howdy, would you look at that!" I said. I thought it was a little suspicious that I was looking at the gun but Jimmy was looking at me. "Do you know anything about this?" I asked.

"No idea."

"Do you suppose it could have been one of the ranchers?" I figured if they'd keep us stocked with shells for killing those pesky rabbits, one of them might have tossed in a gun, too.

"Your guess is as good as mine," he said.

Then a funny thing happened. While I was trying to familiarize myself with the rifle, Jimmy took it from me and started showing me different things about it, things only someone who'd handled it before could have known. I confirmed later with Jimmy Livingston at the hardware store what I suspected—Jimmy bought that gun for me, but he didn't want me to know.

That was Jimmy for you.

Elizabeth Taylor is one of the most beautiful women I have ever met. In fact, outside of my wife, she's maybe *the* most beautiful. When she was eleven years old, she starred alongside Roddy McDowall in *Lassie, Come Home*, but she really burst into the public eye at age twelve, starring as Velvet Brown in 1944's *National Velvet*. Following her role as Amy in *Little Women* in 1949, she made the switch to adult roles, starting with *A Place in the Sun*, where she first worked with George Stevens. Even though Elizabeth didn't get an Oscar nomination for that film, it removed all doubt as to whether she was a bona fide movie star.

I first met Liz when she was doing wardrobe tests at Warner Brothers before we started shooting. Of all the actors in *Giant*, I had the hardest time getting to know her. Being from Texas, I'm a naturally friendly guy. The way I see it, we're all just folks, pretty much all the same. Sometimes that can get me in trouble or nearly get me in trouble—as with Jack Warner and the jackrabbit ears—but for the most part, I get along with everybody. That proved out on *Giant*, where I made good friends with a diverse group of people ranging from Jimmy Dean and Dennis Hopper to Carroll Baker and Mercedes McCambridge.

But Liz was a different story. Right from the start, she was a little standoffish. Maybe it was because I didn't have the same Hollywood pedigree as everybody else or simply because I was just a rodeo cowboy from Texas, but it seemed as if she thought she was better than me. Or so I thought. Of course, now that I look back on it, she *was* better than me. I was just Bob Hinkle from Texas, and she was . . . well, she was Elizabeth Taylor, Hollywood royalty. But back then I didn't know who was better than whom. Hell, I thought I was as good as anybody. I might have even been gutsy enough to think I was as good as she was. Why, I bet she didn't even know how to saddle a horse.

My relationship with Liz was destined to take a turn, though. And neither of us saw it coming until it happened.

One day, I was at the house Jimmy, Chill, and Rock shared, working with Jimmy and Rock on one of the Bick and Jett scenes. We sat in the backyard, facing away from the house, with our shirts off. Just three good ol' boys catching some sun. Liz and Patricia Westmore, her hairdresser, came to the house unannounced. Because we had our backs to the house, we didn't know they were there until Liz's prankster streak took over.

She grabbed a water hose and moved behind us. When she was close enough, she motioned to Patricia to turn on the faucet. That cold spray of water hit us like a bolt of lightning. We squealed like a trio of girls. Jimmy jumped up and ran to the other side of the yard, while Rock beat it into the house. I made a strategic decision: I charged the woman holding the water hose.

Liz shrieked and tried to duck, all the while keeping the hose aimed at me, squirting for all she was worth. I grabbed her arm, but she squirmed away. We were both laughing, but I was the one getting soaked. I lunged again. This time I got a good grip on her arm. I managed to get the hose out of her hands and turned it back on her. Well, Patricia just about died when she saw that. I was about to undo an hour's worth of her hairdressing work. She ran to the faucet, her hands slipping as she tried to get the water turned off, but she couldn't move fast enough. By the time she succeeded, I had soaked Liz head to toe; her hair was plastered to her head.

I thought she looked beautiful.

After we had dried off and cleaned up, we decided to go into town to get a bite to eat. We'd been taking our meals at the hotel, and I was getting a little tired of it. The food was very good, but for most west Texas boys a seven-course meal is a 'possum and a six-pack. After a while I got to hankering for a good old cheeseburger, the kind you can't find in a fancy restaurant. I wasn't sure how the Hollywood stars would feel about that, though.

"Tell you what," I said, "I think I'm gonna get me one of those Texas cheeseburgers at the drive-in. Anybody want to go?"

It was unanimous, and we piled into Jimmy's car. I drove, while Jimmy sat in the passenger seat with Liz between us. Rock and Patricia rode in the back. We headed to the Marfa Drive-In, the 1955 equivalent of today's ever-present Dairy Queen in small Texas towns.

A carhop greeted us with a big smile. "What can I get you folks?" I could tell that she knew who was in the car—other than me, of course—but neither she nor any of the others at the drive-in bothered them for autographs. That was typical of most Marfa folks. They were excited about the movie and loved to see the actors, but they were always very respectful.

Texas gentleman that I was, I deferred to my passengers. "What do y'all want?"

Almost in unison, they asked, "What are you gonna have?"

Well, I was gonna have what I came for: "one of them Texas cheeseburgers." Nowadays we have quarter-pounders and half-pounders and double this or double that or super-size it, but back then you could either get a hamburger or a cheeseburger or a Texas hamburger or a Texas cheeseburger. The Texas ones came with a little bit bigger bun and a little bit bigger patty—just a better deal.

"And I want everything on it," I added. That meant mustard and chopped onions. I wasn't going to be kissing too many women that afternoon, so I figured it couldn't hurt.

Jimmy got the same thing I did, but Rock got something like a chicken salad sandwich and Patricia ordered something offbeat—I don't remember what it was, just that it was something I'd never had and never would. Liz didn't order anything. She'd had a baby a few months earlier, so she was on a diet, trying to get her waist back to normal. I thought it looked pretty damn good the way it was.

Once the food arrived, I chomped into my Texas cheeseburger, and man, it was just as good as I wanted it to be. Liz started looking at my food. I knew she had to be hungry, and it was downright cruel for us to be eating all that good food in front of her.

She leaned over and asked, "Bob, can I have a bite of your cheeseburger?"

Normally, I'm protective of my food. If you want a bite, order your own damn cheeseburger. But when *Elizabeth Taylor* asks you for a bite of your Texas cheeseburger, you give Elizabeth Taylor a bite of your Texas cheeseburger, no questions asked.

I handed it to her and watched as she took a ladylike nibble near where I had taken my first bite. She chewed a bit, then said, "Boy, that really is good." She proved it by taking another bite or two, then she asked for a drink of my sweet cherry lime, yet another Texas experience she'd never had before.

She gave the cheeseburger back to me, and I took another bite, just as close to her bites as I could. Normally, you would take a bite where nobody had bitten yet so you wouldn't get the other person's germs, but I wanted to get all the germs I could from her.

From that time on, Liz and I were buddies. She was a big kisser, handing out kisses the way men shake hands. When she'd come into makeup, she'd give Rock a little kiss and give Jimmy a little kiss. Well, now she included me in her kissing. A few times she even asked me to eat with Rock, George, and her at the hotel. I usually ate with Monte and Chill, so we could cuss and tell jokes and have guy talk and leave the stars and George to talk about whatever stars talk about. When Liz first asked me to eat with them, I didn't feel right about it, so I figured I needed to make some kind of excuse for the boys, something like, "Well, they want to go over some lines, so I'd better go eat with them." I didn't want Chill and Monte to think I was over there kissing the stars' butts.

A few weeks into filming in Marfa, Mike Wilding flew in to visit Liz on the set. Mike was a British actor who was the second (after a short-lived marriage to Nicky Hilton) of eight husbands for Liz (seven if you don't count Richard Burton twice). Turnabout's fair play, I guess; she was the second of four wives for him. In 1979 he died tragically when he suffered an epileptic seizure and fell down a flight of stairs. But Mike was Liz's current husband in 1955 and the father of her two boys, Michael and Christopher.

Liz asked me to ride in the limo with her to the airbase to pick up Mike when he landed. She had told him all about me—I guess a west Texas cowboy might be considered an oddity that just had to be seen by an Englishman—and was anxious for us to meet. When we arrived, a number of folks from the press were already waiting. I suspect someone's publicist, maybe even Liz's or the one from Warner Brothers, put the word out to make sure we were in the headlines.

When the plane arrived, Liz introduced me to Mike, who I really took a liking to. The only problem was that I had a hard time understanding what he said—not so much because of his British accent but because he talked so fast. He seemed to be in a hurry to get his words out and didn't appreciate the Texas tradition of ambling along in conversation instead of racing to the finish. That same Texas tradition applied to listening—we listen in slow motion just like we talk in slow motion, so I had a real problem with Mike about that.

The next day a picture appeared in one of the Dallas papers of me standing between Mike and Liz. The caption beneath the picture said "Actor Mike Wilding, unknown, and Elizabeth Taylor on the set of *Giant* in Marfa, Texas." I still have that picture. I guess when you're with Hollywood royalty, "unknown" is the best you can hope for.

During the time Mike was in Marfa, I met an old boy from Kermit, Texas, named Larry Spruill, who drove down to the set. Folks were always coming out to watch the filming, so the crew had set up a rope about fifty feet away from the cameras to keep them at a distance. Nobody minded them being there, but we didn't want them wandering into any shots.

Larry motioned me over. "I been watching you for a while," he said. "Looks like everybody knows you, so I figure you might be about half-important." To some, that might sound like an odd thing to say, maybe even an insult, but to a Texan it was high praise.

Then he asked, "What kind of transportation do y'all have out here?" Turns out he was a car dealer back in Kermit, and after I explained that Warner Brothers had rented cars for most of the cast but I didn't have one, he said he'd leave me a brand-new 1955 Mercury, one of his dealership's demos, to drive. "You just put gas in it and drive it like it's yours."

In Texas, you have to return hospitality—I think it's a rule, but I can't swear I've ever seen it written down—so I said, "Why don't you come on inside the rope. No need for you to stand out there."

Of course, that's exactly what Larry had wanted all along. Once he made it inside the rope, I introduced him to everybody, and he had a grand old time. He was happy because he got to meet the Hollywood stars, and I was happy because now I had a car of my own. Yes sir, things were going pretty good for ol' unknown.

Larry came back a week or so later. When I saw him at the set, I figured my free-car days were over, but he just wanted to know how it was running. Then he said, "We're gonna have a party in Kermit at the country club. We'd like to have y'all come up there. We'll have all the booze you can drink and a little dancing. Give y'all a chance to get away and have some fun."

When I told everybody about it, the initial response was "yeah, let's do it," followed by "where the heck is Kermit?" They had learned that, in the wide-open spaces of west Texas, you didn't let mileage or location be the deciding factor on anything. After all, nothing is close by, so if distance was a deal breaker, you would never do anything or go anywhere.

The good folks from Kermit sent two limos to pick us up at the end of shooting that Saturday and to carry us to the Kermit Country Club. I rode in one with Rock, Jimmy, and George Stevens, Jr., while Liz and Mike followed in the other. Kermit was about a three-hour drive from Marfa, so it was damn near 10 P.M. before we got there. But as late as it was, you'd have thought we were arriving in prime time at a big Hollywood premiere. Hundreds of people waited out front, with police to control the crowd and traffic, and the ever-present media was there with cameras.

Larry came out to escort us. In what I still consider one of the most gracious acts I've ever seen, Liz let him take her by the arm and lead her in. I guarantee you, at that moment that ol' boy would have written out a check to her favorite charity for any amount she asked because she made him the biggest man in town. He showed up on the front page of the Kermit newspaper, big as life, with Elizabeth Taylor hanging on his arm as he led her through the line of gawkers.

The party went on until about three in the morning, and we had us a grand time. We ended up spending the rest of the night in town. Jimmy, Rock, George Stevens, Jr., and I stayed at Larry's house, while Liz and Mike Wilding stayed across the street at the home of Larry's uncle and business partner, Mark Spruill. The limos took us back to Marfa the next morning. Liz accidentally left a red dress in one of the guest bedrooms at Mark's, and I called Larry several times and asked him to send it to Marfa because Liz really wanted that dress. He kept saying he would, but he never did. I guess it made a pretty good souvenir from Elizabeth Taylor.

CHAPTER SEVEN

Potpourri, *Giant* Style

Look. Cowboys and no cows.
—Drunk cowboy in parking lot

And horses' rear ends and no horses.
—Bob Hinkle

One day Jimmy saw an advertisement about bullfights in Ciudad Acuña, a border town in the Mexican state of Coahuila, just across the Rio Grande from Del Rio, Texas. I've got to tell you, I don't care much for bullfighting. I'd roped 'em, wrestled 'em, and ridden 'em, but just standing out there in a fancy suit and sticking 'em with swords? That didn't appeal to me then and still doesn't today.

Jimmy, however, was really into it, though I'll be damned if I know why. It was only a couple of hundred miles to Del Rio, so I let him talk me into driving down with him on a Saturday evening for the fight (if you can call it that) the next day. When we reached Del Rio, all the motels were full. After considerable looking, we finally found a hotel downtown that had one room available—with only one double bed. We had come too far and were too tired to turn back, so we took it.

After we checked in, we scouted out the town on foot. A car eased over beside us as we left the hotel. I figured it was someone who recognized Jimmy, so we ignored it.

On the set of *Giant* (June 1955). *Left to right:* Dennis Hopper, Monte Hale, Fran Bennett, and Bob. Courtesy of Bob Hinkle.

"Hey boys, I thought I'd find you."

I knew that voice. We turned and looked, and sure enough: it was Fran Bennett. Great (please note the sarcasm)! Just what we needed.

Fran was playing the role of Judy Benedict, Bick and Leslie's daughter. She came from a wealthy family in Fort Worth and had a prep school background, including the exclusive Hockaday School for girls in Dallas. She was young, probably about twenty or so, but her sophistication made her seem a bit older. She was also very pretty, and like almost every young girl in America and certainly like all those in Marfa, she had a crush on Jimmy. She was always doing things for him on the set, like getting him coffee or water, and she seemed to be trying to impress him with her money.

Jimmy liked her just fine, but he didn't give a damn about her money, and he had no romantic interest in her. As soon as we saw Fran, we knew why she was there. Neither of us believed for one minute that she was a bullfight fan. No sir. We knew she was there chasing after Jimmy. Nowadays, I guess you'd call it stalking, but that concept hadn't been invented in 1955.

"I've been driving around for an hour looking for y'all," she said. "I finally saw your car at the hotel, so I've been waiting for you to come outside."

"Well, you found us," Jimmy said.

"I can't find a room anywhere," she said, then paused. I knew she wanted an invitation to stay with us, but I'll be damned if I was going to extend it.

"You may have to look somewhere outside of town," I said. "Del Rio's full up."

"Y'all have a room, don't you?"

"It's not big enough for three," Jimmy said. I could tell by the look on his face that he wanted to say not only "no" but "hell no!"

Fran was clearly disappointed, but she didn't make much fuss. "Well then, I guess I better keep looking."

I don't know where she ended up spending the night, but we didn't see her again until the next day when she found us at the bullfight and sat with us. There's not much to say about the "fight," but Jimmy really enjoyed it. For me, it just reinforced how little use I had for the whole thing. We had a good time, though, and afterward Fran went her way and we went ours.

As Jimmy and I headed across the parking lot, we passed a group of three or four cowboys standing behind a pickup truck. They'd downed more than their fair share of beer, and that usually spells trouble. I think they must have recognized Jimmy because the biggest one—a fellow about my size and age—said as we walked by, "Look. Cowboys and no cows."

"Yeah," I said. "And horses' rear ends and no horses."

He stepped into my path, hands clenched. "What did you say?"

West Texas rule number one of fighting: if it can't be avoided, the best way to win a fight is to land the first blow. My fist connected square with his chin before he had the last word out of his mouth. He dropped like a turd from a tall cow, out cold as a clown before he hit the ground.

Jimmy immediately took off his glasses, stuck them in his pocket, and started after another one. That fellow didn't seem interested, though. He waltzed backward, while Jimmy danced around like a banty rooster—more Baryshnikov than Joe Louis. He got in that ol' boy's face and popped him a couple of times before his opponent skedaddled with his other buddies, who had already scattered like cockroaches.

We went on to Jimmy's car, leaving one cold-cocked cowboy lying in the parking lot. We figured his buddies would come back for him later. Jimmy was downright excited. I think that five-second round got his adrenaline flowing in a way the bullfights never could.

"How'd you do that, Bob? Knock him out with one punch?"

"You've just got to know where to hit him. Back in Brownfield, my buddies and I fought just for the heck of it, for something to do. We never tried to hurt anybody. We just wanted to see who was the toughest, so you'd fight and find out, then you'd shake hands and you were still friends. A few years of that and you learn some things, like where the right button is."

When we reached Jimmy's car, I stepped back and looked him over, head to toe, as if I were appraising him.

"What?" he asked.

"Damn, you're a tough little bastard."

"You're not too bad for a big bastard, either."

From that point on, our nicknames for each other were set: Big Bastard and Little Bastard. Later, he would name the Porsche Spyder he died in "Little Bastard."

Working on those rope tricks came in handy during the filming of one scene in *Giant*. In the movie, Luz is killed when Warwinds, the horse Bick bought from Leslie's family in Virginia, throws her. When her will is read, everybody is shocked to learn that she has given a tiny piece of the Reata Ranch, maybe six or eight acres, to Jett. Bick can't have that, so he and his buddies call Jett into Bick's office to buy him off. That scene really worried Jimmy.

"Bob, what am I going to do? I just sit there while Rock and Chill and Monte put pressure on me. Rock's got the good lines."

Almost from the start, Jimmy was jealous of Rock because he felt Rock had the best dialogue. Ironically, Rock was just as jealous of Jimmy because he thought Jimmy got all the good scenes. I remember one time, before a scene where Jett drives off in that big car and Bick is supposed to stop him, Rock asked me, "How am I going to hold my own with Jimmy in this scene?"

I thought for a minute and said, "The only way I can think of is for you to scratch your nuts." I don't believe he followed that advice. Then again, it's been a while since I watched the movie.

Anyway, Jimmy and I got to figuring out how he could keep from being part of the furniture in Bick's office in that scene. After a minute it hit me. "Take that knotted rope in there with you," I said. "The whole time they're talking to you, just keep messing with that rope. Everybody's going to be watching you, wondering, 'What the hell does he have in his hand? What's he doing?' Then at the end of the scene, when you walk over to the door and tell Rock you're not going to take the deal, pop that rope, give them the 'everything's smooth' signal, and walk out."

I had a little hand gesture I used anytime someone asked me how things were going. I'd hold my hand out flat, then run it straight across in front of me to show that "everything's smooth." That's the signal I was talking about.

When they filmed the scene, Jimmy played with that rope the whole time. At the end he used the hand gesture, smiled, and flat left those other ol' boys, fine actors every one, hanging on the walls. They had to be scratching their heads, trying to figure out how the character with almost no dialogue could be the star of the scene. But Jimmy damn sure did it.

I've talked about what a psychologist George Stevens was, but he didn't limit his psychology to Rock and Liz. He used it on just about everybody, Jimmy included. And it worked like a charm every time.

After Jett turns down Bick's offer to buy him out, there's a later scene where Jett paces off the small piece of land he inherited from Luz. To a Texan, especially a west Texan, land is everything. It wasn't much acreage, but it was Jett's, and he was mighty proud to be a landowner. He names it Little Reata, and in this scene he marks the boundary of his land. It's about more than just measuring the property, though. It's about Jett's pride of ownership and his defiance of Bick. Bick wanted to buy him out, but Jett stood up to him, and now he has his own Little Reata right in the midst of big Reata—a constant reminder to Bick that Jett Rink is still there, alive and kicking.

We finished early one day, and George wanted to shoot that scene before it got dark. It was a simple scene—Jimmy walks right to left, in silhouette against the sky—but it's an important scene. There's no dialogue, so the only crew George took was one prop man and Bill Meller, our cinematographer. Bill won an Oscar in 1951 for *A Place in the Sun* and would win again in 1959 for *The Diary of Anne Frank.*

We got to the location, typical flat west Texas landscape with a windmill, and Bill set up his camera. George pointed to a small ridge and said to Jimmy, "All I want you to do is walk right along there, like you're marking off your land. That's all there is to it."

He called "action," and Jimmy started out across the ridge. He walked nonchalantly, with no attitude in his steps. He had only gotten a few yards when George yelled "cut!"

Jimmy stopped and looked at George for direction. After all, as I said before, that's what directors are supposed to do, isn't it? Direct?

But George just said, "Let's try it again."

Jimmy repeated the scene, but he took bigger steps this time. No nonchalance, just great big old steps. He stopped after about ten yards or so, then looked at George. "Is that what you want?"

"Not exactly."

George motioned Jimmy over to where he and I sat. As Jimmy approached, George ripped a page out of the back of his script, then he tore the page into two- or three-inch squares. Without saying a word, he walked to the ridgeline, bent over and put a square down, then covered it with a rock.

Jimmy and I couldn't take our eyes off him. "What's he doing?" I asked.

"I don't know," Jimmy said.

George went another twenty feet or so and put another piece of paper down with a rock on it. He kept this up until he was a pretty good ways out there. Then he came back and said to Jimmy, "Do you think you can follow those?" Kind of snotty, I thought.

Half PO'd, Jimmy's voice was thick with sarcasm. "Yeah, I think I can."

"Then let's shoot it."

George called "action," and Jimmy walked back to the ridge. But instead of pacing off his land, he picked up the first piece of paper and threw the rock away. He repeated the process on the second and the third pieces until he had retrieved all those squares. He started wadding them up as he came back to us. He held out his hand and turned it over, dumping the wadded paper into George's lap.

"Now look, you're supposed to be the director," he said. There was a distinct edge to his tone. "So direct. Tell me what you want me to do and I'll do it. If I need any marks, I'll put them down myself. But if you can't do that, then I'm going to get on an airplane and go back to Hollywood."

George appraised him for a second. He seemed to be making some kind of decision about Jimmy's attitude. Apparently satisfied, he said, "So you think you can walk it off out there?"

"Just turn that damn camera on and watch me."

"All right, let's shoot it."

When Jimmy got to the ridge, George yelled "action." And Jimmy started marching. I mean *marching*. He stomped along, anger and defiance drumming out of every move because he was royally PO'd at George. Just like Jett is royally PO'd at Bick in the movie. He reached a point, then dug his heel into the dirt to mark it. He kept going, reached an old post that was to be part of the boundary, drew a line in the dirt with his heel, turned, and kept marching. It was a march that would make any West Pointer proud.

"Stay on him, Bill," George said.

"I got him," Bill said, excitement in his voice.

I looked at George, who was smiling. Jimmy was doing exactly what he wanted him to do, and he didn't have to tell him how to do it. It was all Jimmy's idea.

Jimmy Dean on the windmill, on the set of *Giant* (June 1955). Photograph by Richard C. Miller. Courtesy of the Miller Family Trust A. © Miller Family Trust A. All rights reserved.

Jimmy kept going, then he stomped over to the windmill. He climbed up the ladder and just sat there, arms crossed, feet dangling, too PO'd to come down.

"You still got him, Bill?" George asked.

"I got him."

After a few seconds George yelled, "Okay, that's it. Let's go home."

George never said anything else to either Jimmy or me about that scene. Some people made a big deal out of it later, and rumors floated that George and Jimmy had a big blowup on the set, but there was nothing more to it than George ticking Jimmy off so that a ticked-off Jett Rink would give the performance he needed to. Dimitri Tiompkin later put a great score to it, and it made for one helluva scene in the movie. I wish Jimmy could have seen the final cut because I think he would have been damn proud. And as ticked as he was at George that day, he would have appreciated what George had done to bring that performance out in him.

After Jett strikes oil on the Little Reata, there's a great scene where he drives to the main house in his rickety truck, covered head to toe in oil, just to rub Bick's nose in his newfound wealth. In the scene, Rock, Chill, Monte, Sheb Wooley, Jane Withers, and Liz are on the porch of the Benedict house, having a little party or something. Jimmy is supposed to drive down the driveway and park in front of the house, then go up on the porch for his confrontation with Rock.

Jimmy improvised a bit in that scene, some on his own and some at my suggestion, and I think it came out perfect. Jett was supposed to be drunk, so Jimmy decided not to drive straight down the driveway but to run over the grass instead. I thought that was a nice touch, to have the respectable ranchers on the porch look out to see this drunken, oil-covered renegade zigzagging toward them, then plowing up the lawn.

Jett gets out and staggers up on the porch. "My well came in big, so big, Bick. . . . Me, I'm gonna have more money than you ever thought you could have. You and all the rest of you stinkin' sons of Benedicts."

Just as it looks as though Bick is going to jump on Jett, Leslie calms him down. Jett leans back on the porch and looks her over, then says, "You sure do look pretty, Miss Leslie. You always did look pretty. Just pretty nigh good enough to eat."

That was a line I gave Jimmy. It was also the line that touched off the fight between Bick and Jett. It was an old Texas saying you used when something looked pretty damn good to you. It certainly didn't have the same meaning it does today, or it never would have stayed in the movie in 1955. Looking at it now, I guess both meanings work because, either way, it damn sure would have touched off a fight with a woman's husband.

We usually worked six days a week, taking Sundays off, but as the Fourth of July neared, we were going to get two free days in a row for the first time since we'd been filming—Sunday the third and Monday the fourth. A couple of days before the weekend, Liz called me to her dressing room.

"You ever been to Neiman Marcus, Bob?"

"Once. About a year ago."

"I've heard so much about it."

Hell, everybody'd heard of Neiman Marcus. It was one of the most exclusive stores in the country, located in downtown Dallas. Herbert Marcus, Sr., and his sister and her husband, Carrie Marcus Neiman and A. L. Neiman, founded the store early in the 1900s. Herbert was a buyer for the old Sanger Brothers department store in Dallas, and both Carrie and her husband worked for A. Harris and Company at the time. Over the years, Neiman Marcus had become synonymous with luxury, competing with the likes of New York's Saks Fifth Avenue and Bloomingdale's for the high-dollar clientele.

Then came Liz's kicker: "I really would like to see it. Do you think you can arrange it?"

Could I arrange it? Man, I don't know. It's not like she'd asked for a bite of my Texas cheeseburger. "Liz, it's over five hundred miles to Dallas. We'd have to go to Midland to catch a plane, and it's two hundred miles just to Midland." As I said before, in west Texas there are miles and miles of miles and miles.

"I really would like to go." She practically cooed. All that was missing was her batting her eyelashes.

Well, who can say "no" to Elizabeth Taylor? Certainly not me. "Tell you what," I said. "I'll make a few calls and see what I can find out. But I can't make any promises."

We had a single phone on the set, tapped in to Worth Evans's line at his house. Since it was our only line, I had to get permission from the production manager to tie it up. Then I called information in Dallas, got the number for Neiman Marcus, and placed the call.

"May I talk to Mr. Neiman?" I asked the woman who answered.

"There is no Mr. Neiman."

"Who's the head honcho there?"

"That would be Stanley Marcus." Stanley's father and aunt had founded the store.

"Let me talk to him."

She put me through to his secretary, who wanted to know why I wanted to talk to him.

"Warner Brothers is making a picture out here in Marfa, Texas, called *Giant*, starring Elizabeth Taylor, Rock Hudson, and James Dean. Elizabeth Taylor wants to know if she can come to Dallas and visit Neiman Marcus. I'm trying to find out if it's going to be open on the day before the Fourth of July."

"Just a minute and I'll put Mr. Marcus on."

She probably thought it was a prank call, but true to her word, she put Mr. Marcus on. It wasn't a minute, though; it was more like ten or fifteen seconds.

"Normally we're not open on Sundays," Stanley Marcus said, "but I'll open it up for y'all and let you buy anything you want. I'll even send my airplane to Marfa for you."

I guess he couldn't say "no" to Elizabeth Taylor, either.

On Saturday, we finished shooting a big scene a little after lunchtime, then George and Jimmy moved to the oil well to

On the flight to Dallas, Bob tells Jimmy Dean, Elizabeth Taylor, Buddy Van Horn, and Valerie Keen Van Horn what to expect there (July 1955). Photograph by Richard C. Miller. Courtesy of the Miller Family Trust A. © Miller Family Trust A. All rights reserved.

shoot Jett striking his gusher. While they shot that, those of us going to Dallas were getting ready. We had to wait for Jimmy to get cleaned up, not a simple task considering he was covered in the syrup they used for oil. Sure enough, Stanley sent a twin-engine Beech airplane for us on Saturday afternoon. I don't know if it was his personal airplane or if he had chartered it, but he sent his wife, Billie, with it to accompany us. I'm pretty sure he didn't charter her.

Jimmy, Liz, and I made the trip, but Rock stayed behind. My recollection, hazy though it may be after more than fifty years, is that Rock had recently started "dating" Phyllis Gates, secretary to his agent, Henry Willson, and she was coming to

Elizabeth Taylor follows Jimmy Dean and Bob off the plane in Dallas (July 1955). Photograph by Richard C. Miller. Courtesy of the Miller Family Trust A. © Miller Family Trust A. All rights reserved.

Marfa for the weekend. When Rock and Phyllis got married shortly after we finished filming *Giant*, the rest of us wondered what that was all about. We all knew he was gay, something he told me when I first started working with him. Well, actually he told me he was bisexual.

"I hope that won't affect our relationship," he said. Hell, I didn't care. All I wanted to do was teach him how to be a Texan. Rock and I became friends over the course of making the picture, and I had, and still have, great admiration for him. I found him to be a total professional, always a perfect gentleman to everyone.

It took only a couple of hours to reach Dallas by air, and when we arrived at Love Field, Stanley had a limo waiting to

Rock Hudson (June 1955). Courtesy of Bob Hinkle.

Breakfast at Stanley Marcus's house in Dallas, Texas (July 1955). *Clockwise from left:* Billie Marcus, Bob, Jimmy Dean, unidentified man, Liz Taylor, unidentified woman. Photograph by Richard C. Miller. Courtesy of the Miller Family Trust A. © Miller Family Trust A. All rights reserved.

drive us to his huge house in east Dallas. That night he threw a big party, with about two hundred of the richest people in Texas in attendance—and when you're talking about the richest people in Texas, you're talking about *really rich people.*

Liz stayed the night with the Marcuses, while Jimmy and I spent the night with Stanley's neighbor across the street. The next morning we had a nice breakfast at Stanley's house, then we headed to Neiman Marcus. The downtown streets were deathly quiet on a Sunday and a holiday weekend to boot. The limo dropped us off in front of the store, the manager opened the doors and locked them behind us after we were in, and our shopping spree was on.

Jimmy Dean putting in Stanley Marcus's backyard in Dallas, Texas (July 1955). Photograph by Richard C. Miller. Courtesy of the Miller Family Trust A. © Miller Family Trust A. All rights reserved.

Jimmy Dean and Liz Taylor at Stanley Marcus's house in Dallas, Texas (July 1955). Photograph by Richard C. Miller. Courtesy of the Miller Family Trust A. © Miller Family Trust A. All rights reserved.

Back in those days, Texas and a lot of other states had what were known as "blue laws," which prohibited most kinds of shopping on Sundays except for food and other necessities. Because of that, Stanley said they couldn't take cash for any purchases, but he had one of his accounting people set up personal accounts for all of us, then he gave us credit cards with $10,000 credit limits. Can you imagine that? The sum of $10,000 to shop for clothes? Even at Neiman Marcus, where in 1955 ties sold for $35 apiece and suits started at $200, I couldn't imagine spending that kind of money on duds. I could get a helluva suit for $39 or $49, and I could buy two Cadillacs with $10,000 and still have money left over to buy a bunch of suits. What was I going to do with ten grand

Liz Taylor and Jimmy Dean in Stanley Marcus's backyard in Dallas, Texas (July 1955). Photograph by Richard C. Miller. Courtesy of the Miller Family Trust A. © Miller Family Trust A. All rights reserved.

in a department store? By the time we left, I think Liz had spent only about $1,500. Stanley gave me a tie, and I did buy some Neiman Marcus–brand perfume for Sandy, but that was about it for this ol' boy.

The next stop was Fair Park, home of the State Fair of Texas, the biggest state fair in the country. I suggested we go because some time back I had ridden a giant wooden roller coaster there, an experience I wanted the others to share. I'm still trying to figure out how we got in because the fair was in the fall, and I'm sure the park must have been closed that Sunday. Somebody, maybe Stanley, made a phone call on our behalf. There were a handful of midway workers but few other customers, and we pretty much had the place to ourselves. We

Jimmy Dean and Liz Taylor on the midway of the State Fair of Texas, with the Cotton Bowl in front of them (July 1955). Photograph by Richard C. Miller. Courtesy of the Miller Family Trust A. © Miller Family Trust A. All rights reserved.

On the midway of the State Fair of Texas (July 1955). *Left to right:* Billie Marcus, Liz Taylor, Jimmy Dean, and Valerie Keen Van Horn eat watermelon. Photograph by Richard C. Miller. Courtesy of the Miller Family Trust A. © Miller Family Trust A. All rights reserved.

rode that roller coaster several times, and Jimmy and I spent a lot of time at a shooting gallery, blasting at ducks. I remember a few other games as well, like throwing balls at stuffed kittens and playing pinball. There was a lady who made hats out of straw, and she gave hats to Jimmy and Liz to wear. We had a blast.

I'll never forget that: Fourth of July weekend, 1955.

A few days later, filming wrapped in Marfa. Warner Brothers chartered a train to haul us back to Hollywood, along with our gear and equipment. George had signs made in the shape of Texas, with a marker for Marfa, that bore the names of the movie and the stars and put them on both sides of the box-

At the State Fair of Texas (July 1955). *Left to right:* Liz Taylor, Bob, Stanley Marcus, and Jimmy Dean playing pinball. Photograph by Richard C. Miller. Courtesy of the Miller Family Trust A. © Miller Family Trust A. All rights reserved.

cars. The train was going to be a rolling advertisement for the movie all the way across the southwestern United States.

Everybody was supposed to be checked out of the hotel by noon, but it ended up taking all day to load the train, so we had a lot of free time to kill. Jimmy and I knocked around town, saying farewell to the good folks of Marfa who had done so much to make our stay comfortable. As the time got near for leaving, Jimmy and I sat with Clay Evans in his car and talked until it was time to go. We had become close friends with Clay, even though he was younger than we were. He had rodeoed some, so I naturally gravitated to him while we were there.

Saying good-bye was sad because we had really enjoyed our time in Marfa and had met some of the nicest people in the world. When you spend virtually every day with people for

Billie Marcus and Liz Taylor watch Jimmy Dean shooting in an arcade on the midway of the State Fair of Texas (July 1955). Photograph by Richard C. Miller. Courtesy of the Miller Family Trust A. © Miller Family Trust A. All rights reserved.

three months, they become almost like family, and we knew we would miss them. I stay in touch with some of those folks and still consider them friends. But as sad as I was about leaving the good folks of Marfa, I was looking forward to seeing my family again. Sandy and I traded letters and talked on the phone occasionally, but three months was the longest we'd been apart since we'd been married. I couldn't wait to get back home to her and the kids.

Jimmy and I were about the last ones to board the train, at around seven that evening, and it started for home. They must have taken all the whiskey out of Texas because I had never seen so much booze. Jimmy and I only had a couple of

Liz Taylor and Billie Marcus, eating cotton candy on the midway of the State Fair of Texas (July 1955). Photograph by Richard C. Miller. Courtesy of the Miller Family Trust A. © Miller Family Trust A. All rights reserved.

beers, but Chill drank enough for all of us. The trip was pretty much a twenty-four-hour party for most folks, but not for Jimmy and me. We reminisced about our time in Marfa and talked about our future plans together.

Little did I know that I had only about two more months left with Jimmy.

CHAPTER EIGHT

That's a Wrap

If a man can bridge the gap between life and death, if he can
live on after he's dead, then maybe he was a great man.

—JAMES DEAN

W e arrived back in Hollywood on a Friday, had two days
off, then went to work on Monday at Warner Brothers.
It was also a chance to get back to our personal lives after
being away for so long. Jimmy was moving to Sherman Oaks,
so on my twenty-fifth birthday, July 25, 1955, I borrowed a
pickup truck from the studio to help him. After the move, we
ate dinner at my house, where Sandy cooked Jimmy's Texas favorite: chicken fried steak and mashed potatoes with gravy,
topped off with apple pie for dessert. Jimmy missed his home
in Indiana, and he had adopted us as a second family. He
loved coming to our house to play with the kids and to have
some good home cooking. And let me tell you, Sandy could
flat do some home cooking.

I was recently at Warner Brothers, so just for grins I went
to the archives and looked at the call sheet for July 25, 1955.
It reflected that the production manager had loaned Bob Hinkle a pickup to move James Dean from Hollywood to Sherman Oaks. Funny how something that trivial is still
memorialized after all these years.

July 1955 was also when Jimmy ordered his Porsche 550
Spyder. As I noted before, he had blown the engine on his

Porsche Speedster in a race in Palm Springs while he was filming *Rebel Without a Cause*, and it had been in the shop all these
months. Jimmy had ordered a bigger engine that had to be
shipped from overseas, which is why it took so long. When the
car was finally ready, about the first of August, I drove Jimmy
to Competition Motors on Highland Boulevard to pick it up.
While we waited, Rolf Wutherich, Jimmy's friend and personal
mechanic, said, "Let me show you something."

He led us to a brand new Spyder in a small showroom. It
had just arrived, fresh from the factory, for another customer.
Jimmy slid behind the wheel, probably imagining what it
would be like to drive it. It was love at first sight for him. I
could easily predict what he'd say next, and he didn't disappoint: "I want one of these."

Jimmy wasn't earning much by Hollywood standards,
about $1,500 a week under his contract with Warner Broth-
ers, but he paid $3,000 cash and traded in his Speedster for
the new Spyder that Rolf ordered. And just like that, Jimmy
bought his death car.

When it arrived a few weeks later, we immediately took it
for a spin. I crammed my six feet two inches into the passenger side, and Jimmy headed up Highland, then cut over to
Mulholland Drive. On Mulholland's bends, Jimmy opened it
up. He grinned from ear to ear, laughing and acting like a
kid. He particularly enjoyed making the tires squeal as he
raced around the curves. I didn't say anything to him, but I
wasn't that impressed with the Spyder. It was noisy, had very little room, and sat so low you could reach out the window and
touch the ground. If I'd known what the Spyder's ultimate
fate, and that of its driver, was going to be, I really would have
hated it.

"Man," I said, "six thousand dollars for a car and it doesn't
even have a trailer hitch."

"If we do any rodeoing, we'll pull the horse trailer with
your Cadillac," he said.

We both got a good laugh out of that—maybe the only laugh I ever got out of that damn car.

The notion of us rodeoing was another of our little jokes, but it almost got Jimmy in hot water with Warner Brothers executives. As we had in Marfa, we set up bales of hay at the studio and kept practicing our roping. A reporter from one of the trades was watching us practice one day, so we decided to put on a little show. We had no idea how gullible he would turn out to be.

Jimmy swung the rope around his head, then made a perfect toss, dropping the lasso right around a bale. "Oh yeah. We're gonna do all right when we get to the Cow Palace." The Cow Palace in San Francisco was one of the biggest stops on the rodeo circuit.

"I got us a couple of good horses," I said. "Yes sir, we're going to do just fine."

We went on like that for a bit, just a little harmless fun—we thought—pulling the reporter's leg, but damned if he didn't write an article that said Jimmy and I had entered as a roping team at the Cow Palace. Nothing against Jimmy, but if I had any intentions of entering the team roping competition, I would have chosen a professional for my partner. As good as Jimmy had gotten, he wasn't *that* good. Anybody who knew anything about rodeo should have dismissed the article out of hand.

But the studio honchos bought it. They were convinced we were going to be riding bulls or bucking broncos or doing something dangerous like catching bullets in our teeth and that Jimmy would get hurt. They didn't give a damn about me; I was just Bob Hinkle, dialogue coach from Texas, but James Dean was their golden boy. They got hold of his agent, Dick Clayton, pronto, to put a stop to Jimmy entering the Cow Palace rodeo. Like any good agent, Dick immediately came to the studio to talk to Jimmy, who set him straight. We had another good laugh, but we learned our lesson about messing with reporters: when they want a story, they won't let the facts get in their way.

Things weren't all fun and games for Jimmy, though. He was in the middle of negotiating a new contract with Warner Brothers, so he was feeling pressure. Back in those days, actors didn't have the freedom to make whatever deals they wanted to for individual movies with producers because they had contracts with the studios. They could only make the movies their studio told them to. It's a lot like football players' contracts with their teams. As long as they're under contract to a team, that's the only team they can play for. One difference was that sometimes studios would "loan" actors to other studios—for example, MGM had loaned Liz to Warner Brothers for *Giant* and Universal had loaned Rock—but the studios still dictated the financial terms.

Jimmy asked me several times if I knew what other stars, such as Marlon Brando, were making and who the highest-paid actors in town were. In 1955, Liz and Rock were the tops in the business, both getting around $100,000 for *Giant*. Jimmy felt he was contributing as much to the movie as they were and he shared top billing, so he couldn't understand why he was making only $1,500 a week. That might seem like a lot of money, especially for 1955, but it wasn't when compared to the money his costars were making.

Early one morning, assistant director Joe Rickards called Jimmy into makeup, with plans to shoot one of his scenes at nine. As it turned out, they didn't get to his scene that morning. That wasn't unusual on *Giant* because the assistants had a bad habit of bringing actors to the set in anticipation that George might get ahead of schedule—which almost never happened—and they wanted the actors readily available. They didn't seem to understand, although they should have, that getting ahead of schedule was rare but falling behind was commonplace. That resulted in a lot of idle time for actors who could have been doing other things.

Jimmy and I took a long lunch that day, then they sent him back to makeup. After that, it was sit and wait again. I stayed close to the set while Rock filmed some scenes, but I periodically checked with Jimmy in his dressing room. I found him growing more agitated each time. "Bob, what the hell are they doing?" he'd ask. "When are they going to get to me?" I never had an answer. Finally, about 2:30 or 3:00, Joe Rickards went to Jimmy's dressing room and said, "Doesn't look like we're going to get to you today. You might as well go home." Without a word to anyone but ticked to the gills, Jimmy cleaned off his makeup, changed out of his wardrobe, and left.

The next morning Jimmy was set for an early call, but he phoned me and said, "I'm not coming in today. I'm going fishing." I knew Jimmy liked hunting rabbits, but fishing? That was a new one on me. His next words cleared it up: "They made me wait all day yesterday. Today they can wait on me."

Ahhh, not going fishing as in *going fishing* but going fishing as in *taking the day off.* It would put me in a tough spot because I was going to be the first person they questioned when Jimmy no-showed. Sure enough, about midmorning Joe Rickards came looking for Jimmy. The trick in a situation like that is to answer the question without answering the question. That way you don't have to lie, but you also don't have to tell everything you know.

"I haven't seen him," I said.

"He was supposed to be here at nine o'clock."

"That's not my department."

See how nicely I dodged the question?

After checking with everybody, Joe called Jimmy's house, but with no luck. I knew Jimmy wouldn't answer because he and I had a code worked out. If I needed to get in touch with him, I would call, let the phone ring one time, then hang up and call right back. Otherwise, Jimmy wasn't going to answer. A few minutes later, though, someone came along who I couldn't lie to or mislead.

"Bob," Liz asked, "where's Jimmy?"

"He's ticked off because they didn't get to him yesterday."

As soon as I said that, Liz got ticked off, too—at Jimmy. "He can't do that," she said. "That's not professional. He's got all these people waiting on him. He can't take it out on these innocent people who are just trying to do their jobs."

I saw her point. It takes a lot of people to make a movie, and most of them aren't high-paid stars. When production shuts down because someone refuses to work, it hurts the hardworking crew more than it does the studio. Remember how Joan Crawford was jealous of Mercedes McCambridge on the set of *Johnny Guitar* because Mercedes was so popular with the rest of the cast and crew? The widely reported story was that Mercedes's popularity stemmed in part from the fact that she was so efficient at filming her scenes that on her shooting days they usually finished early. Joan's days often dragged late into the day and sometimes into the night. There's an old saying, "One monkey doesn't stop a show," but one monkey was stopping this one. And the crew of *Giant* would remember that it was James Dean who held them up that day.

"Get him on the phone," she said.

I called, using our code, and gave the phone to Liz. She proceeded to rip him a new one. I was afraid my hair would get burned from being so close to her flames. She ended with, "Bob and I are coming to get you."

Jimmy lived about ten minutes away, on Dickens Street. When Liz and I got there, he was in a good mood, notwithstanding Liz's tongue-lashing. He was tickled that he had gotten his point across.

"Jimmy, you can't do this," Liz said.

"I've got to teach them a lesson. They can't just drag me over there and then have me waste my whole day."

"The way you get even with them is by getting into their pocketbook. You demand another fifty thousand dollars on your next movie, and you make sure they know what it's for. Once you get big—and you're going to be really big—you can demand anything you want, and they'll give it to you. But you don't punish a bunch of innocent people."

I could see that Jimmy was starting to feel a little bad about what he had done, so he agreed to follow us back to the studio. When we got there, George took Jimmy into his dressing room to have his own talk with him. I don't normally eavesdrop, but I'll admit to standing outside and listening through the air vents over the door. George got a little rough, and I suspect Jimmy was ready to go back to work—even if he had to sit and wait all day—just to be through with the lectures he was getting.

"You're going to be a major star in this business," George said, echoing Liz. Then he dropped the other shoe. "But you're not a major star yet." And he wasn't. *East of Eden* was Jimmy's only starring role to date. *Rebel Without a Cause* hadn't been released, and we weren't through shooting *Giant*. One successful picture does not a career make.

"You're starting off wrong in this business by pulling something like that," George continued. "No matter how good you are, people are going to be reluctant to work with you if they think you're hard to work with. You don't want to get that stigma attached. The business is bigger than any of the stars. Don't ever forget that."

And that was pretty much the end of that. When George found out the reason for Jimmy's stunt, he made sure it never happened again. For his part, Jimmy promised George that any time he needed him, "Just give me an hour's notice, and I'll be ready." They kissed and made up (figuratively, of course), and the show went on.

Everything Jimmy did in front of the cameras seemed natural and easy, but it only looked that way because he labored hard at his craft. The whole time we worked together on *Giant*, I saw him struggle only once. It was the scene toward the end where Jett Rink gives a drunken speech at a banquet to celebrate the opening of his new hotel. The character of Jett had been inspired in Edna Ferber's novel by Texas wildcatter and oil tycoon Glenn McCarthy, known in the media as "Diamond Glenn" and the "King of the Wildcatters." This particular scene was based on the big bash McCarthy threw in 1949 to celebrate the opening of his $21 million (in 1949 dollars) Shamrock Hotel in Houston, an event Houstonians will still tell you was the biggest social affair in Houston's history.

For some reason, Jimmy couldn't get that scene down. George had the actors rehearse it for days—literally. We would be doing something else on set or shooting a different scene, then at the end he would call us over to rehearse that banquet scene yet again. One time Jimmy tried it by really being drunk. He had booze brought to the set and drank enough to get tipsy—not so drunk he couldn't act, but enough to create the effect he wanted. It worked too well. His speech was so slurred that you couldn't understand him. But after all that, he finally got the scene down and George shot it.

That was Jimmy's last scene.

When movies wrap, the cast and crew often give each other mementos of their time together. Sometimes they're gag gifts, sometimes not. Chill and I gave Jimmy a stuffed armadillo as a reminder of Texas. Rock and Liz gave me a St. Christopher's medal, even though I'm not Catholic. The inscription on the back simply says "To Bob, from Rock and Liz." I later gave the medal to my daughter, Melody; I don't believe she'd take a million dollars for it.

At the beginning of the shoot, makeup takes pictures of the backs of the male actors' heads as a record of how long their hair is and how the hairline looks so they can keep it consistent throughout the shoot. Chill got hold of those pictures and took them around, getting the actors' autographs. My most precious gift came from my friend Jimmy. After shooting his last scene, he called me to the middle of the set, where he held a sack and a picture. I recognized the picture immediately. It was an 11 × 14 black-and-white shot of Jimmy that had been hanging on the wall in the Green Room. He had taken it down without asking and presented it to me. But I most remember and cherish what was in the sack, a replica of an Oscar with this inscription: "Robert Hinkle. I owe this character to you. You created it. Many thanks. Your friend, James Dean."

Jimmy had given me his friendship, a rifle, and now an Oscar. Today, that Oscar is in the James Dean Museum in Fairmount, Indiana.

It would be the last thing he would give me other than memories.

CHAPTER NINE

Oh, Bury Me Not

Live fast, die young, and have a beautiful-looking corpse.
—James Dean

September 30, 1955.

Jimmy had finished his last day of shooting on September 17, but life carried on without him on the set. He had been back a few times, doing some looping and other technical work, but he was pretty much on his own for a while. My phone rang fairly early the morning of September 30. I looked out the window as I picked up, taking in a beautiful fall day.

"Hey, Bob," Jimmy said. "I'm headed to Salinas for the race. See if you can get off and go with me."

Jimmy's contract with Warner Brothers said he couldn't race while principal photography was ongoing on *Giant*, but now that his part had ended, he was raring to go. He and I had talked several times about the race in Salinas, in Monterey County, and I really wanted to make the trip with him. Though I didn't like the Spyder, I was anxious to see him race it. He had painted his racing number, 130, on the doors and hood, and on the back, where the motor was located, he had painted the words "Little Bastard."

I knew that Jimmy really wanted me to pull his custom-made trailer with the Spyder on it. He had bought a brand-new 1956 Ford station wagon about a week earlier so he'd have something to pull the trailer. With my experience towing horses to rodeos, I was a natural to haul the car.

"Let me check with Tom. I'll call back around eight."

Tom Andre, our production manager, said George wanted me to work with Rock on some looping. Looping is essentially redoing lines that got covered up in the original shooting or hadn't been clear. The reason can be anything from outside noises to slurring of words. The process is simple, but it can be very time-consuming. The actor has to watch short portions of the scenes over and over on a "loop" while trying to repeat the lines exactly. A lip-synch, in effect. The goal is to glean at least one usable effort for the film.

I knew looping with Rock would take most of the day, so I called Jimmy and begged off. "I hate for you to have to go up there alone," I said.

"Don't worry about it. I think I can get my dad to go." Jimmy's dad, Winton Dean, lived in Santa Monica, and Jimmy was trying to reconnect with Winton despite his dislike of his stepmother.

"Be sure and call me if you win," I said. "And good luck."

We hung up, and I started going over the lines Rock needed to loop. He was due around ten o'clock, and I wanted to be ready. Little did I know then the surprises the day held in store for me.

Shortly after I arrived at the studio, Chill, who was doing some looping of his own, stopped by my office, carrying a small antique rocking chair. It almost looked like a child's toy in his hands.

"Where'd you get that?" I asked.

"Just a little gift from one of my many admirers."

"What are you going to do with it?"

"Well, the first thing I'm going to do is take it home after I get through looping. Then I'm going to clean up, put some toilet water on, and you and me are going to the game."

I couldn't believe I had nearly forgotten about the game. Bear Bryant and his number-one–rated Texas A&M football team were in town to play UCLA that night. The Bear had come by the studio a couple of days earlier with soon-to-be Heisman Trophy winner John David Crow and linebacker Jack Pardee in tow. The publicity department had arranged for Bryant and the two players to visit the set, figuring it was good publicity for a film about Texas to have Texas legends there for photo shots. Besides, we Texans—like Chill, Monte, and me—always pulled for Texas teams, whoever they were.

Chill had met Bryant before, but that was my first time. He was a big ol' boy, about my size, wearing his trademark houndstooth hat. I had played football in high school, defensive back and end, and Bryant was a hero of mine, just as he was to virtually every Texas high school football player. I was awestruck meeting him, something I never felt even with the biggest Hollywood star.

"How many tickets do you boys need for the game?" Bryant asked Chill.

"Just two, for Buckle and me," Chill said. All I could do was nod.

Bryant reached into his coat pocket and pulled out two tickets in the front row, right behind the Aggies' bench.

"You boys enjoy the game."

After Chill left my office with his chair, I spent the next few hours with Rock. Jimmy called a couple of times to keep me updated on his trip. He said his dad couldn't go but that Sandy Roth, an independent photographer for fan magazines, would be going along to take some photos.

"I sure hate to let him drive my new station wagon," Jimmy said.

I didn't blame him. Roth and his wife had taken me to dinner a few weeks earlier to talk about a story he was doing on Jimmy, and he about scared the dickens out of me driving to the restaurant. He may have been a helluva photographer, but steering a car in a straight line was challenge enough for him. Pulling a car on a trailer would up the ante beyond Roth's meager means.

"You know," I said, "Bill Hickman's been wanting to go. He can drive that station wagon."

Hickman was a stuntman who had worked on *Rebel*. He would later become one of Hollywood's best and most well-known stunt drivers and coordinators, with driving credits on such films as *Bullitt*, *The French Connection*, and *The Seven-Ups*. I gave Jimmy Hickman's number and hung up. The next time I heard from him was around noon. He called to tell me he had Hickman with him as well as Rolf Wutherich, his mechanic who had ordered the Spyder for him. Jimmy said they were gassing up both cars before leaving.

"I'll call you tomorrow and tell you how we did," he said.

That was the last time I ever spoke to him.

Chill called around five o'clock that afternoon. "Buckle, I'm on my way. Meet me by the gate." I was with George, Rock, Liz, Jane Withers, and Carroll Baker in the projection room, watching rushes from the previous day's shooting, so I left them and went to the gate. As I killed time talking with the guard, the head of publicity for the studio, Bill Hendricks, drove onto the lot in his new Mercedes. I could tell immediately from the look on his face that something was wrong.

"Did you hear the news, Bob?"

I hadn't heard anything that would have painted a long face on me like the one on Bill. "What?"

"I just heard from one of the wire services that Jimmy Dean got killed racing his car in Pasa Robles."

The words made no sense to me. Sometimes we Texans talk slow so our brains can process the words before we say them. That's the problem with some of the fast-talking Hollywood types; our brains have to go into overdrive to process the words as fast as they come out.

"Bill, that race is in Salinas, not Pasa Robles. And it's not until tomorrow."

Now he seemed confused. "Let's go up to the office and get on the phone. We gotta find out."

Damn straight we did! I knew, just *knew*, Bill was mistaken. But there was still that nagging doubt in the back of my mind. What if he was right? I knew Jimmy had to go through Pasa Robles to get to Salinas. I also knew he'd be testing the Spyder on some of those winding roads. And he did like to drive fast.

I jumped in Bill's Mercedes, and we drove to his parking space near his office. I took the steps two at a time to the second floor, with Bill hot on my heels. He had called ahead and gathered three or four others from the publicity department to meet him there. The office reminded me of a newsroom, with several desks clustered together. Bill's office was at the back and, in true Hollywood executive style, was plush, the walls adorned with pictures of movie stars.

"Bob, call up to Pasa Robles and get the number of the funeral home," Bill said. "If it's true, that's probably where they would have taken him. Maybe you can find out something there."

My hands shook as I called directory assistance and got the number. I hesitated before I dialed. As long as I held off, as long as we had no confirmation, then it couldn't be true and Jimmy wouldn't be dead. I felt every eye in the place on me as I finally dialed, slowly, carefully.

"This is Bob Hinkle at Warner Brothers Studio," I said to the man who answered. "Can you tell me anything about an automobile accident involving Jimmy Dean, the actor?"

"I'm sorry, sir, but we can't give out that kind of information."

"Can you just tell me if he's been brought to the funeral home?"

"I'm sorry, sir, but no, I can't."

Something about the way he said it told me there was substance to the news Bill had brought. If they can't give out that kind of information, that meant there was, in fact, information. In turn, that meant something had happened, and it had involved Jimmy. My heartbeat kicked into overdrive. I felt sweat at my temples.

"Is anyone there from Warner Brothers?" I asked.

"There's a gentleman named Bill Hickman."

I didn't like hearing that. If Hickman was there, that meant Jimmy was there. "Let me talk to him."

When Hickman got on the line, his voice was choked with emotion. I knew before he said the first words that it was true. "Bob, Jimmy's dead," Bill said.

"What the hell happened?"

"When we got to Bakersfield on Forty-Six, Jimmy had me pull over so he could take the Spyder off the trailer. He said he wanted to fine-tune it before we got to Salinas. He and Rolf got in it and they ran it a bit, then he'd pull over and tinker with the engine a bit. I just followed them." He laughed, but there was no joy in it. "Hell, he even got a ticket for going seventy in a sixty [mph zone]. Anyway, we were just outside of Pasa Robles when some kid coming the other way tried to turn left in front of Jimmy and hit him head-on. Jimmy never had a chance. Rolf got thrown out of the car, and he's in critical condition."

I felt the blood drain from my face, then my breathing came up short. I felt as if I was going into shock. After I hung up, I looked at the folks gathered in the office.

"Jimmy's gone."

I called over to the projection room and asked for George Stevens. Everyone knew he hated to be interrupted when he was working, so I told the operator it was an emergency. After a few minutes, George came on the line.

Jimmy Dean, on the set of *Giant* (1955). Courtesy of Bob Hinkle.

"What's going on, Bob?"

I could tell from his tone that he knew something was wrong. He knew that I knew it had to be a real emergency for me to interrupt him. He was probably thinking something had happened to George Jr., his son, who was in the air force and flew a lot more than his dad was comfortable with. George lived in constant fear that George Jr. would be involved in a plane crash, so the word "emergency" probably hit him hard. Unfortunately, although I could assure him on one count, I couldn't reassure him on another.

"George, Jimmy's dead," I said. "He was killed in a car wreck near Pasa Robles."

"Are you sure?" he said. Disbelief filled his voice.

I assured him that we had checked it out and that there was no mistake. I told him how Hickman had said it happened, then we fell silent for a moment. I could tell he was having as hard a time digesting the news as I was, and neither of us could offer the other any comfort.

"Where are you now?" he asked at last.

"At the publicity department."

"Come over here and let's sort this out."

I hung up as the numbness started to wear off. Somewhere during my conversation with George, the first tear leaked out.

George, Rock, Liz, and Carroll were waiting outside the projection room when I got there. The sound of hearts breaking was almost audible. When they saw me, faint traces of hope returned to their faces. Everybody had the same question: are you sure? As if there were a chance it was just a rumor and Jimmy was still alive.

Liz seemed particularly upset, almost in hysterics. She grabbed me around the neck, sobbing. "No, no, no! Tell me it can't be true. Tell me he isn't dead."

I wanted to give her that reassurance, but I couldn't. All I could manage was, "Yes, I'm sure." I explained that I had talked to Bill Hickman at the funeral home in Pasa Robles, and there was no mistake.

Somebody had called Mike Wilding for Liz, and he arrived about then. Though he had been called to pick up his wife, he hadn't been told what had happened. The sight of Liz and the rest of us wandering about in a state of shock baffled him. He held her in his arms and tried to console her, but she wouldn't be consoled.

He looked at me. "What happened?"

And so, yet again, I spoke the words I hated hearing, hated saying. As the truth settled on all of us, emotions began to subside, but they only burrowed under the surface, deep into our souls.

"Bob, you and Mike have to go to Jimmy's house and make sure it's locked up," Liz said through her tears. "You need to check on Marcus." Marcus was a small cat she had given Jimmy.

I nodded, unable to speak through my tears. I gave Liz the key to my office so she could have privacy while Mike and I were gone, then we got into Mike's car and drove to Sherman Oaks. Poor Mike was almost beside himself, first having to console his wife, and then having to console a blubbering cowboy in the car beside him. "Everything's going to be all right," he said, over and over.

But it was a lie.

Jimmy lived in a small guesthouse behind a larger residence. It was more like a bachelor pad than a house, in effect an efficiency apartment. Almost all of Jimmy's *Giant* salary went into his cars and motorcycles, so the two-hundred-dollar monthly rent on the guesthouse suited him. He had just completed his negotiations with Warner Brothers, and his new contract would pay him one hundred thousand dollars per movie, based on two movies a year, for the next five years. No doubt he would have been moving out of the guesthouse shortly, but now that was not to be. Neither was his next movie going to happen for him, *Somebody Up There Likes Me* for MGM as the tradeoff for MGM having loaned Elizabeth to Warner's for *Giant*. Instead, Paul Newman would play the lead in the role that would make him a star.

Jimmy had left one window open, I guess for circulation. The place was so small it was hard to tell if anything was out of order. It was furnished meagerly with a small Formica table and two chairs, a tiny black-and-white TV set, and a bed, and there was very little room to move about. There was some mail on the table, and his clothes were strung around the place. For all we knew, it had either been ransacked or was exactly as Jimmy had left it.

As we looked for Marcus, my thoughts were as broken as my heart. I thought of the times I had been there with Jimmy, going over lines in the script, laughing, and planning our futures. Sometimes actress Ursula Andress had been there, too. Jimmy was very taken with Ursula—I think he was in love with her and just didn't know it. I was teaching her Texan and she was teaching me German, and this tiny guesthouse was our schoolroom.

After about fifteen minutes, Mike and I concluded that a neighbor was keeping Marcus until Jimmy returned from Salinas. Now I guessed the neighbor would be keeping him permanently.

We closed the window, locked the door, and returned to the studio at around eight o'clock.

The mood had not changed. Liz knew that Jimmy and I had been particularly close, and she sensed the depth of my loss over everybody else's. She took my hand and led me away from the group while Mike went to my office to make phone calls. The others drifted their separate ways.

Liz and I walked to the sets on the back lot where Jimmy had worked. We must have looked a sight, the most beautiful woman in Hollywood and a west Texas rodeo cowboy walking hand in hand, joined in our emotions. The more she tried to console me, the harder I cried; the more I tried to console her, the harder she cried. I think we simply fed off of each other's grief.

"Do you remember the very first scene you did with Jimmy?" I asked. "The one where Leslie asks Jett to drive her to the Mexican village?"

She laughed through her tears. "I remember that when he said his line, 'Old Bick wouldn't like that,' I ad-libbed, 'F—— Bick, I'm in charge down here.'"

We both laughed. "Jimmy was really nervous doing that scene with you," I said. "That broke the tension for him."

We laughed until we cried again, then continued our rounds. We returned to my office around nine or ten o'clock. There was nothing else to say, no words of comfort left to convey, so we headed our respective ways. Sandy was waiting up for me when I got home. We talked long into the sleepless night about Jimmy and how at home he always seemed to be, playing on the floor with our kids. But Jimmy would never be in our home again, would never eat at our table again, and would never hit Mike in the head with a rope again.

Sandy held me in her arms, and I wept.

Production was quickly drawing to a close. We were going a little over budget, so George wanted to finish as quickly as possible. We were scheduled to shoot the next day, which was a Saturday, but Liz got sick and so George shut down the production. I don't know if Liz was physically sick or emotionally sick or both, but she was in no shape to work. I don't guess any of the rest of us were either.

Jimmy really liked Liz, and he always spoke very highly of her. He was almost in awe of her; she was a mighty big star in his eyes. I think the feeling was mutual. Even when Liz chewed Jimmy out for skipping work, she made it a point to let him know how convinced she was that he was destined for great things in the business. For a while, I was pretty sure something would develop between Liz and Jimmy during the filming, but it never did.

The following Monday Liz still couldn't work, so we tried to shoot around her. It wasn't until Wednesday that she was able to return, and even then none of us had our hearts in it. When you spend that much time with someone and grow as close as we all had, it's impossible to simply shut off the emotions and conduct business as if nothing has happened. But we were professionals, and we had a job to do, so we pressed on like good soldiers. I think we all wanted this to be a great movie as a final tribute to Jimmy.

Ironically, that last scene that Jimmy had so much trouble with, the drunken speech at the banquet, continued to be a problem even after Jimmy was gone. In a way, I felt like it was Jimmy staying in touch, reminding us that even though he was gone, he wasn't really gone. While editing the scene, George realized that Jimmy's words were so slurred that some of them were unintelligible. I guess he made a pretty good drunk after all. Unfortunately, good drunks don't make for clear dialogue. George called me to watch the footage with him, and I saw right away what his concern was. I thought I might have a solution, or at least a partial solution.

"When Jimmy was rehearsing I recorded him," I said. "I've still got the tape where he practiced these lines."

You would have thought I'd just promised George an Academy Award. I hustled to my office and got the tape. We were able to pull some words and partial sentences from it to dub into the scene, but it still wasn't enough. Now we were really in a bind. No one wanted to say the obvious because the last thing any of us wanted to do was dwell on the fact that Jimmy was gone. Someone came up with the idea of approaching Nick Adams to help out.

Nick was a young actor just starting out in the business. He was later best known for his role as Johnny Yuma in the television series *The Rebel*, but he'd also had a small role in *Rebel Without a Cause*, where he and Jimmy became close friends. One of Nick's claims to fame was that he did a pretty good impersonation of Jimmy, right down to his voice, so we dragged him over to dub some of Jimmy's lines and finally got everything worked out.

As an interesting side note, Nick and Jimmy were two of four actors from *Rebel Without a Cause* who died tragic deaths, leading to a superstition in some circles that the cast of *Rebel* was "cursed." Nick died in 1968 of a drug overdose. Some say it was a suicide, while others claim he was murdered. Sal Mineo was stabbed to death at age thirty-seven in the alley behind his West Hollywood apartment in an attack some say had a "homosexual motive," while conventional wisdom says it was merely a botched mugging. Natalie Wood tragically drowned in 1981 when she fell off her and her husband, Robert Wagner's, yacht anchored near Catalina Island. Also onboard was actor Christopher Walken, but neither man missed her until it was too late.

They took Jimmy's body to Fairmount, Indiana, for burial, but none of the *Giant* cast was able to attend his funeral because we were still shooting. Henry Ginsberg, George's producing partner, was the sole representative from the production. Even if I had gotten off work, I couldn't have brought myself to go, not even to be a pallbearer. I wanted to remember him the way he was the last time I saw him, laughing and carrying on and having fun. I wanted to remember hunting jack-rabbits with him and sending the ears to Jack Warner. I

Bob at Jimmy Dean's headstone in Fairmount, Indiana (2005).
Courtesy of Bob Hinkle.

wanted to remember him popping knots through ropes or las-
soing hay bales. I wanted to remember him playing "Cattle
Call" on his guitar and fighting drunks in a Mexican parking
lot at bullfights. I wanted to remember him on the State Fair
of Texas midway, shooting ducks in a gallery and wearing straw
hats. I didn't want to remember him as a casket that couldn't
be opened.

Jimmy and I had talked a lot about what we hoped to ac-
complish in our lives. We talked about where we had come
from and where we were going. He shared secrets with me
that I don't know if he shared with anyone else. He had been
in love with the Italian actress Pier Angeli, but her mother

wanted her to marry Vic Damone, which broke Jimmy's heart. He told me about his fling with Natalie Wood while they were filming *Rebel*, and he revealed the sordid truth behind the rumors that he was a homosexual: the Hollywood casting couch wasn't just about starlets and male producers; sometimes, as in Jimmy's case, it was about male actors and male producers who didn't care about an actor's sexual orientation. You do what you have to do to succeed. That explained the curious remark Jimmy had made months earlier about the FAGGOTS— STAY OUT sign posted at Barney's Beanery: "That's why I like to come here."

Jimmy's mother died of cancer when he was just nine years old, and he felt abandoned when his father, Winton Dean, sent him to live with an aunt and uncle. I think that's why he so enjoyed coming to our house for dinner with Sandy and the kids—there, he could be part of a family. Jimmy talked about forming his own production company, so he could write and direct as well as act. He wanted me to be a part of his company and to help him find projects to develop. Although I have had a wonderful career, I sometimes wonder how it might have been different had Jimmy not taken that trip that day. What would he have become? What would I have become?

Where would I be today?

PART III

New Opportunities

CHAPTER TEN
_____

Texas Connections

Now that is a stuntman. That's perfect; one take. I've never
shot a stunt where we could do it in one take.
                    —ANDRE DE TOTH, DIRECTOR OF *RIDING SHOTGUN*

My rodeo background always seemed to stand me in good
stead in the picture business, particularly when it came
to doing stunts. In those days, when you signed up to work at
the various studios, they had you fill out a card listing the
kinds of stunts you could do. In addition to my great ability to
fall down, I listed things like "rope calves" and "bulldog
steers." One day, before my gig on *Giant*, I got a call from a
casting director at 20th Century Fox who wanted to know if I
could do a "bulldog." She had no idea what a bulldog was or
what it meant, and she didn't know the difference between
bulldogging a steer and bulldogging a man. All she knew was
that she had a sheet that called for someone to "bulldog," and
my stunt card had that word on it.

This was for a biblical-era picture called *The Robe*, starring
Richard Burton, which was released in 1953. I couldn't figure
out why they needed a rodeo stunt in a movie like that. It
turned out to be an example of a casting director not knowing the difference between bulldogging a steer and bulldogging a person, but that worked to my advantage. In the movie,
Burton's character rides up to a bridge, but a fellow on a horse
is blocking folks from getting across. Burton's character has to

bulldog that guy off the horse to clear the way. By the luck of having an ignorant casting director, I ended up doubling for Richard Burton in that scene.

In 1954, Bob Ellsworth at Columbia Pictures called and asked, "Can you buck off of a horse?"

I said, "I've never seen a horse I couldn't buck off of." What I didn't do too well was actually *ride* bucking horses, but getting thrown off? I was your man.

So Bob booked me on a picture called *Riding Shotgun*, being filmed at Big Bear, in San Bernardino County. Andre de Toth, a native of Austria-Hungary who had obtained a law degree from the Royal Hungarian University before getting into the picture business, directed this B western that starred Randolph Scott. Another familiar-to-be-but-not-yet-familiar actor in the picture was Charles Buchinsky, who later changed his name to Charles Bronson. I was hired to double for Jim Millican, who had been playing character roles in movies since the early 1930s.

The studio arranged for a limo to drive me to the set all the way from Los Angeles, a hundred miles or so, even though it was just for one stunt. I suppose the experience should have prepared me for the later limo ride to see Rock Hudson, but it didn't. When I got to the set, every eye was on me. And what eyes they were. There was a corral set up for the scene, and sitting on the top rail, as extras, were some of the best rodeo cowboys in the world: Jerry Ambler, former world saddle bronco riding champion; Gerald Roberts, former all-around world champion; Wag Blessing, former bull riding world champion; and Larry Finley, former bareback riding champion. You can imagine how I felt. Here I had been called out to do a stunt on a bucking horse, and my audience was going to be a group of guys who would know every mistake I made, probably even before I made it.

"Here's what I want you to do," the director said. "That horse is going to buck a couple of times, then I want you to fall off right in front of the camera. We're going to have it set up to shoot under that bottom rail on the fence. Got it?"

"Yeah, I got it." I didn't think it sounded too hard. I knew I could ride that horse for at least two jumps, and I knew about where I'd buck off. But there was that audience of experts that was going to be watching. Not just experts—*critics.* Then again, they were experts at *riding* horses, but I was the expert at falling off.

I got on the horse, and the director said "go."

The camera rolled and—boom, boom, plop—two bucks and a perfect fall later, the scene was over. The director said "cut," then announced to the boys on the top rail, "Now that is a stuntman. That's perfect; one take. I've never shot a stunt where we could do it in one take."

He went on and on, almost embarrassing me. I didn't have the heart to tell him it was more luck than talent that controlled the whole event. I thanked him graciously, got in the limo, and rode back to Hollywood. I'd earned an easy $350 and left all those cowboys wondering just what in the hell had happened.

After *Giant,* I decided I was going to quit doing stunts and extra work and concentrate on being an actor. Even though I hadn't acted in the picture, I had spent all day every day with some of the best actors in the business, and I had stood shoulder to shoulder with one of Hollywood's finest directors. I had seen the making of a movie from start to finish. If that wasn't the best possible education for an actor, I don't know what was.

Unfortunately, just saying you're an actor doesn't necessarily make you one. The acting parts were few and far between at first, but over the years I started getting more and more roles in several popular television westerns, such as *Gunsmoke, Wyatt Earp, Wells Fargo, Tombstone Territory, Bonanza,* and *Wagon Train.* I needed the work, too, because our little family was growing. In September 1956 our third child and first daughter, Melody, was born.

My experience on *Giant* also helped get me work in ways other than acting. In 1956, I got a call from the casting office at MGM, where they were making a picture called *The Opposite Sex*, with Joan Collins—*Dynasty*'s Alexis Carrington Colby—and June Allyson. In the movie, actor Jeff Richards was supposed to play a Texan, so they turned to ol' "unknown" to work with him. I ended up spending about two months on that picture, all of it shot at MGM.

I also managed to find a few roles on the big screen, mostly uncredited, during the first year or two after I finished *Giant*. In 1955, I played the uncredited Jake in *The Far Horizons*, a movie about the Lewis and Clark Expedition. Fred MacMurray played Meriwether Lewis, Charlton Heston played William Clark, and Donna Reed was Sacajawea. That was back in the days when all the big stars were Anglo-American, and they played the major roles in pictures, regardless of what ethnicity the characters were supposed to be. How else do you explain Charlton Heston playing Mexican police chief Ramon Miguel Vargas in 1958's *Touch of Evil* or John Wayne playing Genghis Kahn in *The Conqueror*? I'll talk more about that last one later.

The next year I played the uncredited Lieutenant Hargrove in *The First Texan*. Doesn't that title sound like the lead role was made for me? Instead, Joel McCrea played Sam Houston. Also in 1956, I had an uncredited part as Joe in *Dakota Incident*, starring Dale Robertson and Dallas's Linda Darnell. Yet another uncredited role gave me the chance to meet one of history's wealthiest and most mysterious men.

Howard Hughes acquired control of RKO Studios in the late 1940s. One of the last movies made at RKO, before it was shut down after Hughes sold it to the General Tire and Rubber Company in 1955, was *The First Traveling Saleslady*. Conventional wisdom says the movie was such a flop that it helped

On the set of *The First Traveling Saleslady* (1956). *Left to right:* Harry Cheshire, Ginger Rogers, Bob, and John Eldredge. Courtesy of Bob Hinkle.

speed up the closing of RKO, but not for want of a great cast: it starred Carol Channing, Ginger Rogers, Barry Nelson, and James Arness, who was just starting to make a name for himself with *Gunsmoke*. It was also one of the first credited movie roles for Clint Eastwood, with whom I became close friends during the filming. Arthur Lubin directed the picture. He had directed the Francis the talking mule pictures, in which Chill Wills did the voice of Francis, and later directed such popular television shows as *77 Sunset Strip, Maverick,* and *Bonanza,* not to mention that all-time film classic *The Incredible Mr. Limpet.*

At the close of shooting one day, Arthur told us, "If you're not working tomorrow, don't come over here. We're going to have a closed set." That was mighty unusual, but who was I to question it?

I was working the next day, and when I showed up I found out what the big secret was. Howard Hughes was coming to the set to see Ginger Rogers, with whom he had once been romantically attached. Our instructions were simple: "Don't say anything to him, don't try to shake hands with him, don't bother him, don't do anything. If he says something to you or looks your way, just nod your head and go on about your business."

Everyone except Ginger was nervous, wondering when he'd arrive. Then all of a sudden there he was, just as I finished a scene with her where I testified on the witness stand about how the barbed wire she sold my rancher boss had cut up a calf. As soon as Ginger saw him, she lit up like a Christmas tree. To my surprise, she grabbed my hand and dragged me his way.

"Come on, Bob, I want you to meet Howard."

I didn't know what to do. I didn't want to be disrespectful to Ginger, but the powers that be had been pretty specific—don't talk, don't shake, don't nothing. It sure looked like Ginger was angling me toward "something." She and Howard greeted each other like the old friends they were, with a hug and a kiss. You could tell he was glad to see her by the oversize grin on his face.

"Howard," she said, "I want you to meet this young guy. He's from west Texas."

I should have known that that would get his attention because Howard was also a Texas boy. He was born in the Houston area and attended Rice University before dropping out of school, getting married, and moving to Los Angeles. Didn't he know how important an education was to success? No wonder he never made anything of himself.

"Where in west Texas are you from?" Howard asked.

That wasn't something I could answer with just a nod of my head, like we had been told. I took a chance and broke the rules. "I'm from Brownfield, out in Terry County," I said.

"Hughes Tool Company sells a lot of drill bits out there. Did you ever hear of our bits?"

"Yes sir. I worked in the oilfields, and we used a lot of those Hughes drill bits."

"I'm glad to hear it."

Later, after Howard and Ginger had finished visiting and he was leaving, he looked my way and said, "If you get back to west Texas, be sure and use those Hughes drill bits."

"Yes sir, I sure will."

That was about all I had to say to Howard Hughes, but it was more than most folks ever got to say to him. At least I got to meet him.

Although the luck in my career was good more times than not, those "not" moments made the good ones seem even better. One of them occurred during the filming of *The First Traveling Saleslady*. At the same time we were making that picture, a producer/director named Charles Marquis Warren was preparing a pilot for a television series, a western that was going to be called *Rawhide*. Warren had produced a couple of seasons of *Gunsmoke* and was later executive producer on *The Virginian*, so he obviously knew what he was doing. He came to our set one day to talk to director Arthur Lubin about the new show.

"There are two guys here you better take a look at," Arthur said, when he found out the show was going to be a western. "They're both good horsemen and pretty fair actors."

With that, Arthur introduced Clint Eastwood and me to Warren, who asked us both to drop by his office and leave a picture. Nowadays you'd call it a head shot, but back then it was just a picture. I was there the next day with my mug shot in hand. Warren and I visited for a bit, and I filled him in on some of my background herding cattle, compliments of growing up in west Texas. I knew how to dehorn them, cut them, vaccinate them—just about anything you needed done to or with cattle, I could do. He seemed to think I was a perfect fit for his show, which was about cattle drovers.

"You'll be hearing from me," he said. I walked away feeling pretty good about my chances.

Three days later, things were kind of slow on the *Saleslady* set, so I decided I'd drop in on Warren and say "hi." We'd seemed to hit it off pretty good, and, as with Jack Warner at Warner Brothers, I figured being friendly wasn't out of the question. Some folks would call it a "courtesy call," but others would say I was being a typical Texan, going over and brown-nosing. I soon found out that Warren fell into the latter camp.

When I got to his office, his secretary stopped me. "Do you have an appointment?"

"No ma'am. I just wanted to stop by and say hello."

Behind her, through the door, I saw Warren lean around the side of his desk. When he saw it was me, he said, "Have him come on in."

So far, so good, I thought.

"Sit down," he said, when I entered his office.

He had a bunch of pictures thumbtacked to a corkboard on the side wall. There, among several other actors' pictures and right next to Clint's, was my smiling mug. Even better.

Warren got up and walked to the corkboard. Slowly, almost ceremoniously, he took my picture down, then handed it to me.

"I'm not gonna need this," he said. "I had you in mind for one of these cowboys, but since you've come over here bugging me, I'm not going to use you."

It seems that, unknown to me, Warren had a reputation—not unlike Jack Warner's—of being a jerk, and my courtesy call left me out in the cold on *Rawhide*. My buddy Clint went on to star as Ramrod Rowdy Yates in the show, a role that launched him to a successful career that continues to this day. I'd like to think I could have been there with him.

I later heard another story involving Warren and my friend Dub Taylor that made me smile. Dub had been in countless movies and television shows by the time he worked on *Tension at Table Rock* in 1956, a western Warren was directing. Dub found out that Warren sometimes went by the nickname "Bill." As he passed Warren on the set one day, Dub said, "Whattaya say, Bill?"

Warren tore into Dub. "Don't you ever call me that. You don't know me well enough to call me Bill. Do you understand that?"

Dub responded, "Bill, you can kiss my a——," then turned and walked off.

I don't think Dub lasted much longer on that picture, but he lasted longer than I did on *Rawhide*.

Also in 1956, I worked on a picture in St. George, Utah, called *The Conqueror*, starring John Wayne and Susan Hayward. This is the movie I mentioned earlier in which Duke played the unlikely role of Genghis Khan, and Dick Powell, the actor, was directing. I played Monk, one of Khan's lieutenants as he led his Mongolian hordes across Utah—I mean, northeast Asia.

Once while setting up a shot, Duke pointed out a hill and said to Dick Powell, "That would be a good shot to have me leading all these men off the hill."

When Duke said it would be a good shot of "me" leading the men off the hill, what he really meant was that it would be a good shot of "my stunt double Chuck Roberson" leading the men off the hill.

Powell agreed, but one of the assistant directors piped up, "Chuck's with the second unit."

I figured that left two options: wait for Chuck, or send someone to fetch Chuck. It looked like Duke was leaning toward the latter as he glanced around and his eyes fell on me.

"Hey Bob, come here."

Then I learned there was a third option. "Go to wardrobe," he said, "and put on my outfit, then come back and lead that bunch off the hill. And when you do, I want you to lead them over and under." That meant whupping that old horse from one side to the other, racing down the hill.

I got the wardrobe on, then rejoined Duke and Powell, who seemed to totally defer to Duke on setting up the shot. That wasn't unusual when dealing with stars of Duke's stature. He gave me his last bit of instruction. "When you come off that hill, I want you to really come down hard."

"If we do that, we may lose some of those boys behind me. That's a pretty steep hill."

"I don't give a damn. That'll make it look good. It'll make *me* look good." That last line explained why Powell deferred to Duke on the shot. Sometimes it's all about making the star look good.

We set up the shot, and here I came as instructed, tearing down that hill. My horse was striding about ten feet with each gallop until the hill got too steep, then he slid on his back feet the rest of the way down. Four or five of the guys behind me fell off their horses and nearly got trampled, but we got the shot in. I have to say, it looked pretty damn good. I looked pretty damn good. I mean, *Duke* looked pretty damn good.

Word got around that I had doubled for Duke and that the scene had turned out great, and Chuck Roberson started getting nervous. Job security is only as good as what you're doing right now. That night at supper, Duke called to Chuck, who was sitting across from me at the table.

"Hey Chuck, do you still have any of my wardrobe?"

"Some of it."

"Well, get it to wardrobe so they can alter it to Hinkle's size."

I thought Chuck was going to choke. I thought I was, too. I didn't want to take Chuck's job away from him. I just wanted to do my job. Then Duke started laughing, and we all knew it was just a joke. I don't think Chuck thought it was too funny, but he laughed with the rest of us.

For me, though, it was just one more instance of being in the right place at the right time.

I saw a casting notice one day in 1957 for a television show called *The Sheriff of Cochise*, starring John Bromfield as Sheriff Frank Morgan of Cochise County, Arizona. It was a contemporary crime drama, but they had an episode with some rodeo scenes in it, and that's what they were casting for. The notice specifically said that no one over six feet tall could work on the show, I guess in deference to the star's short stature. Well, I wasn't about to let my six-feet-two-and-a-half inches disqualify me if I had the chops for the part, so I answered the call and met with the producer, Mort Briskin.

"How tall are you?" Mort asked.

"I'm five feet fourteen-and-a-half inches."

He made a note on his pad, gave me a script, and I got the job. A couple of days later, while we were on the set, Mort approached me with a serious look on his face. "You lied to me," he said. "You told me you were under six foot tall."

"No, I didn't."

"Bob, don't lie to my face. I wrote it on my pad."

I said, "Do you still have that pad?"

"Yes, I do."

"Well, you take a look at it and tell me what it says."

He turned and walked away. He returned about thirty minutes later, this time with a bemused smile on his face. "I'll be damned," he said. "I wrote down five foot fourteen-and-a-half. You deserve to be on here for having that kind of nerve."

Guts and BS. Rarely fails.

In the fall of 1956, a fella named Bob Womble, who was one of the largest car dealers in west Texas, had big plans for his Oldsmobile dealership in Lubbock when the new models came out. He had seen Chill Wills on a March of Dimes telethon and decided it would be a crackerjack of an idea to have his own telethon on a local station with Chill as his spokesperson, hawking Oldsmobiles. In exchange for a new Olds, Chill would get to utter such memorable lines as "We'll take anything as a trade-in, even a team of mules." And Jimmy thought Rock got all the good dialogue.

Chill agreed, with one condition: "You've got to bring my manager in, too." I wasn't really Chill's manager, but he saw it as a chance to get me a free visit home. He and I would drive back to Los Angeles after the telethon in Chill's brand-new Oldsmobile. Womble agreed, and the telethon was on.

When we arrived in Lubbock, I learned that, as Chill's supposed manager, it was my job to line up the music for the telethon. In west Texas that meant only one thing: a country music band. There was no shortage of country music bands in Lubbock, but as I scouted around, I kept hearing about this one kid who played regularly at the skating rink. I figured where there's smoke, there's fire, so I brought the kid in to interview. When I first saw him, I almost rejected him on the spot. I expected boots, jeans, and a cowboy hat, but what I got was horn-rimmed glasses, slacks, and loafers. He looked like your typical high school kid, not like a country singer. Still, I couldn't discount word of mouth that said he was real popular in Lubbock, and popular was what we needed because we wanted to draw a big, live crowd of Oldsmobile-buying fans to the telethon.

"You do country?" I asked him.

"Oh yeah. Anything you want."

I was still skeptical, but I made the deal with him, and the telethon was on. I crossed my fingers, hoping he'd at least show up wearing boots and a cowboy hat—he didn't—and that he'd pull in a big audience—he did. Boy, I mean he really packed them in. Boots and hat or not, batting five hundred wouldn't have been too bad except for one thing: most of the audience he pulled was high school kids. As Bob Womble rightly pointed out, high school kids don't buy cars. While we had a good crowd, we didn't have enough buyers to make the telethon worth it for him. Though my experience finding a band for the telethon wasn't that successful, I do pride myself on recognizing talent when I see it. Buddy Holly and his band, the Crickets, went on to a pretty successful career after their stints at the skating rink and the telethon, even though, like Jimmy's, Buddy's career was tragically shortened. I didn't get to know him well, like I did Jimmy, but he was a nice kid. I liked him. Maybe it really is true that only the good die young.

While we were in Lubbock, I took Chill to Brownfield to meet my grandma and grandpa, who lived in a tiny two-room house with an outhouse in back. One of the rooms doubled as a living room and bedroom, while the other was the kitchen/dining room/den/everything else. Chill sat on the bed while I sat on a bench next to my grandma's piano, and we visited for a long time.

My grandma and grandpa died the next spring, on the very same day. I'm glad I got to do something exciting for them before they went, even if was only to bring a part of Hollywood into their house for a very short visit. Until the day she died, my grandma would tell anyone who came to visit, "Chill Wills sat right there. He came in this house, and he sat right there."

CHAPTER ELEVEN

Finally, a Big Hit
in Brownfield

Ohhh, I'm just sitting here, looking and wishing.
—Elderly black man in Brownfield, Texas

I finally got one of my first credited movie roles in 1958 in a picture called *No Place to Land*, in which I played the role of Big Jim. While I got to put my Texan skills into practice in *Giant*, in this one my days of flying Stearmans back in Brownfield were about to pay off. The movie, shot in Hopeville, California, was about crop dusters. Albert Gannaway produced and directed the picture, which starred John Ireland, Mari Blanchard, and Gail Russell. I knew of Gail from some of her pictures with John Wayne. There was also a young actor named Bill Blatty, who would go on to become famous as a novelist under his full name William Peter Blatty. Who can forget *The Exorcist?*

I had never dusted crops before, but the planes they used in making the picture were Stearmans. Some days I'd go to the set and talk to the pilots who had been hired for the flying scenes. Sometimes I would climb inside one of the planes and just sit, my mind going back to my teenage years in west Texas.

In the movie, one of the characters, despondent over the death of a friend in a plane crash, decides to give up flying.

When everyone pressures him back into action, he climbs into a plane and takes off. Once he gets up, he's supposed to do a spin, loop into a couple of snap rolls before diving toward the camera, pass over the hangar, and then disappear on the other side, where he crashes. Beyond the hangar, out of the camera's view, they had an old airplane on the ground, loaded with gasoline, that they would blow up to simulate the crash. The cameras would capture the fireball over the hangar.

There was only one small problem: none of the pilots could do stunts or acrobatics. It seems to me that might have been the key question before they were hired, but apparently it got overlooked. The pilots refused to even try. "You don't have spoilers on the plane," one of them said. "It's too dangerous."

Albert Gannaway was PO'd. "Damn it, what am I gonna do? I can't have a guy just fly around a bit and then crash. If he doesn't do any stunts, it won't be exciting."

"I can do those stunts," I said.

Albert didn't believe me at first. "You telling me you can fly that airplane?"

"Yeah, I can fly it."

He turned to the owner of the planes. "Is it all right if I let this actor fly one?"

Those words must have struck fear into the man's very soul. He also apparently had the soul of a lawyer. "I want a written guarantee that you'll pay me twenty thousand dollars if he crashes." I noticed he didn't mention anything about my funeral expenses. He just wanted to cover the cost of a new plane, plus maybe a little something extra.

Albert also didn't seem concerned about my funeral. After all, there was now money on the line. "Bob, you sure you can fly it?"

"Hell yeah, I can fly it." I wasn't just saying that, either. I *could* fly it, and I knew it.

"You got a deal," Albert said to the owner. "If he crashes, I'll pay you twenty thousand." Then to me, "Go get ready."

The first thing I did was check the gas. I needed just enough to get me through the stunts, but I didn't want to be weighted down. And if, God forbid, I crashed, I didn't want to create my own fireball, though that might eliminate the need for a funeral. The camera crew got the cameras set up, four of them in different places, and off I went. Once up in the air, I felt the same sort of freedom I had felt flying over west Texas. This was just like doing that all over again.

I started with a spin that merged into a loop, then I snap-rolled out of it. I was showing off instead of following the script. I guess I hadn't learned anything from being grounded all those years ago. At the bottom of another loop I did a slow four-point roll, then fell off toward the cameras, diving low. I bounced my tires along the ground by an irrigation ditch, then pulled up into a hammerhead stall. In a hammerhead, you pull up, roll off to one side, then flip the tail up and start back down. I figured it would look good for the cameras.

I then headed toward the hangar for the big "crash." I made a dry run first, close enough to scare some of the camera crew, who were sure I really was going to crash. There was a windsock on a pole next to the hangar, and it must have looked to them as if I was going to hit it, the hangar, or both. I rolled the plane on its side and threaded the needle, but they still scattered. One of them jerked a camera over as he took off.

By the time I had finished the stunts, landed, and taxied to the hangar, the engine quit—out of gas. I was the talk of the set after that. Albert rented the plane for an extra couple of days and had me take nearly everybody up, one at a time, for a joyride. The near consensus was concise: "Bob, that scared the hell out of me."

I say "near consensus" because one of the actors, a guy named Johnny Carpenter, challenged me. "You can't scare me in that damn thing," he said. Johnny had spent the early part of his career doing stunts, including some horse riding in *Na-*

tional Velvet, Elizabeth Taylor's star-making picture. I guess he thought that, as an old stuntman, there wasn't anything or anybody who could scare him.*

Here's where my knowledge of the Stearmans came in. The seats in those things move up and down about a foot or so, worked by a lever. You're supposed to raise the seat before you get in, then pull the lever and it snuggles you into the plane once you're seated. While Johnny was getting ready for his ride, I lowered the seat in front, then tied a shoestring to the lever and ran it back to where I sat in the rear. A few minutes later, Johnny got in and off we went.

I took it easy at first. I wanted him to feel safe and cocky, sort of lull him to sleep. Then, when he wasn't ready for it, I rolled the plane upside down. I could see the veins in his neck stand out, and he gripped the sides of the plane, holding on for dear life. Not scared, my rear end!

And now for the pièce de résistance or, as we would say in Texas, the piece of resistance. I yanked on the string and

---

*Johnny had also written and produced a couple of low-budget westerns, including *I Killed Wild Bill Hickok,* with Denver Pyle, and *Outlaw Treasure,* where he played the lead in a picture in which he was the best-known actor in the cast.

I played the role of Frank James in *Outlaw Treasure,* one of my first speaking parts—and I did it for nothing! I had been working on a picture for 20th Century Fox called *Broken Lance,* with Spencer Tracy, making about one hundred dollars a day, but the role of Frank James had actual dialogue. I thought *Outlaw Treasure* was going to give me my big break. As it turned out, the part wasn't much, and the picture was even less of anything. Amazingly, though, four guys from Brownfield, Texas, had parts in that picture: Allen Thomason, Jack Eicke, Dale Miller, and me.

Another bit of interesting trivia, which might have been of particular interest to the boys from Brownfield—had we known it at the time—is that the female lead in *Outlaw Treasure,* Adele Jergens, started as a Rockette in New York City and got her first big acting break as an understudy for Gypsy Rose Lee in the Broadway show *Star and Garter* in the early 1940s. We may have been from a small town in Texas, but we knew who Gypsy Rose Lee was.

On the set of *Dragnet* (1958). *Left to right:* Warren Parker, Jack Webb, Bob, Gene Roth, and Ben Alexander. Courtesy of Bob Hinkle.

pulled that lever. With the plane upside down, when that seat popped about a foot it must have felt like it had broken and was falling out. Poor ol' Johnny; I almost felt sorry for him. Almost, but not quite. I suppose it might seem a little mean, but he issued the challenge, not me.

After we landed, I saw him hustling over to wardrobe. I guess he had to change his drawers.

I first met Natalie Wood when *Rebel* was winding down and I had started working with Jimmy to prepare for *Giant*. He took me to the *Rebel* set to meet a bunch of the cast, including Sal Mineo, Nick Adams, Dennis Hopper—and Natalie. She and Jimmy were good friends, and she often visited him on the set of *Giant* when we were filming at Warner Brothers, so I got to know her pretty well. She was only seventeen, but she had been acting since she was four or five and was already an accomplished actress.

In 1958 she married Robert Wagner. In the fall of 1959 they signed up to do a movie together for director Michael Anderson, who was still basking in the glory of *Around the World in Eighty Days*, which had won five Oscars—including best picture—four years earlier. The movie was called *All the Fine Young Cannibals* and was loosely based on the life of jazz trumpeter Chet Baker. The real Chet Baker was born and raised in Oklahoma, but the fictional Chad Bixby and his girlfriend, Sarah, were supposed to be Texans.

Shortly before *Cannibals* was to go into production, Robert Wagner called. "Natalie and I are getting ready to do a picture where we're playing Texans, and she wants you to work with us. Are you available?"

"Yes sir." Even if I hadn't been, I would have said yes.

"Can you come to our house right now?"

Less than an hour later, I knocked on the front door of their house in Beverly Hills. They lived on Beverly Drive, one of the exclusive town's main streets, in a house befitting stars: a big two-story house, guesthouse, swimming pool—almost the stereotype of movie star living. The house's previous owner had been Natalie's William Morris mega-agent Norman Brokaw, from whom they had recently bought it for ninety thousand dollars.

I hadn't seen or heard from Natalie since before Jimmy died, other than seeing her at a premiere, but when she opened the door she hugged me as if we'd been friends for a hundred years. Then she introduced me to her husband.

"Robert, it's good to meet you," I said, shaking his hand.

"Call me R.J.," he said. And just like that, it was as if we were old friends.

I worked with Natalie and R.J. for about three months on *Cannibals*. It wasn't the greatest picture ever made, but I enjoyed working with the two of them. That's also when I met

On the set of *All the Fine Young Cannibals* (1959). *Left to right:* Robert Wagner, Natalie Wood, and Bob. Courtesy of Bob Hinkle.

George Hamilton, in one of his first big parts. Our paths would cross again years later in a little disagreement having to do with Evel Knievel. Let's just say I'm not a big George Hamilton fan, but I'll talk about that later.

R.J.'s character Chad Bixby, like the real Chet Baker, grew up dirt poor and played jazz trumpet in the black section of

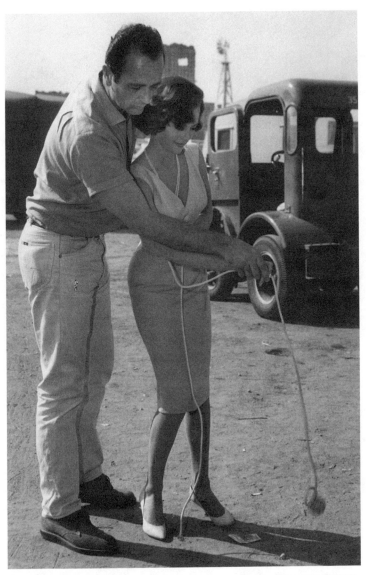

Bob and Natalie Wood, on the set of *All the Fine Young Cannibals* (1959).
Courtesy of Bob Hinkle.

On the set of *All the Fine Young Cannibals* (1959). *Left to right:* Robert Wagner, Natalie Wood, and Bob. Courtesy of Bob Hinkle.

his town. Some of the folks involved in making the movie were sitting around the set one day, talking about a "black section" as if such a thing existed only on the moon. Back then, Los Angeles wasn't as segregated as it is today, so no one knew much about things like that. It makes you realize how sheltered some folks are.

"We've got one in my hometown," I said. I thought I was just making conversation until Michael Anderson, the director, said, "Would you be willing to take Mr. Wagner there over the weekend and show him what those people are like?"

Years later, "those people" would not be an acceptable way to refer to blacks, but this was before the civil rights movement. Even the so-called enlightened folks and liberals were still mired in the dark ages.

So R.J. and I headed for Texas one weekend, my first trip home since the Oldsmobile telethon. The closest we could get to Brownfield by plane was Lubbock, but a couple of my buddies, Jack Eicke—who, as mentioned, had worked on Johnny Carpenter's *Outlaw Treasure*—and Pat MacMillan, picked us up at the airport. Pat ended up driving us the whole weekend, so we didn't have to rent a car.

You can imagine how it turned Brownfield, Texas, upside down when Bobby Hinkle showed up with Robert Wagner. Nothing I had done before made me a big shot in my home-town like bringing a movie star of R.J.'s stature all the way from California did. Not even Chill Wills measured up to Robert Wagner. From then on I was no longer just "Bobby Hinkle" to the good folks of Brownfield; after that, I was Robert Hinkle, the movie star.

The section of town R.J. wanted to see was what locals called "the Flats." Main and Brownfield streets intersected in the middle of town. Going north on Fifth Street took you to the proverbial other side of the tracks, then known as the "col-ored" section. As was the case in a lot of small, segregated Texas towns, most of the homes in the Flats were nothing more than wooden shacks, usually only one or two rooms. I don't recall a single structure that came close to resembling what white folks would consider a real house. There was also a club called Herbert's, where folks gathered to drink. Brown-field was dry, but the police didn't bother with Herbert's much. Ironically, Herbert, the owner, lived in a real house in the white section of town, but even it was better suited for what most Brownfield citizens would call "poor white trash."

We took a lot of pictures for the set designers, and R.J. made notes for his own benefit. At one point, as we drove down the main road through the Flats, with shacks on one side and cotton fields on the other, we saw an old black man— must have been about seventy years old—sitting on the edge of his front porch. He had his head buried in a big book. I'd

In Brownfield, Texas (1959). *Left to right:* Jack Eicke, Robert Wagner, Clarence Hinkle, and Bob. Courtesy of Bob Hinkle.

seen that hundreds of times before, but I knew it had to be a new one on R.J.

"Do you know what he's doing?" I asked.

"Looks like he's reading the Bible."

"No, that's a catalog. Maybe Sears or something. He's wishing."

"Wishing?"

"Yeah, wishing."

"What do you mean?"

"Well," I said, "that's what poor people do. They go through the catalogs and look at pictures and they say, 'I wish I had this' and 'I wish I had that.'"

You'd have thought I'd knocked R.J. upside the head with a hammer. The idea was as foreign to him as it could be. "You're kidding me."

"Let's go talk to him."

Pat stopped the car, and R.J. and I walked over to where the old man sat. He looked at us as we walked up. He didn't have a television and damn sure didn't have money to waste on movies. He didn't see a cowboy and a movie star; he only saw two white men.

"Excuse me, sir," I said. "My name's Bob Hinkle, and this here's Robert Wagner."

"Pleased to meet you," he said, very much a gentleman.

"We saw you sitting over here and wondered what you're doing."

"Ohhh," he said, a big smile on his face. "I'm just sitting here, looking and wishing."

R.J. exchanged a look with me, as if to say, "My education is complete." It was a real eye-opening experience for him.

That was the day Hollywood came to Brownfield, Texas— 1960.

A funny footnote occurred during the filming of *Cannibals*. In the story, Ruby—the character played by Pearl Bailey—dies, and there's a scene of her funeral. Redd Foxx, best known years later as Fred Sanford in *Sanford and Son*, had an uncredited role as Redd, the piano player, at Ruby's funeral. The mourners, all African Americans, were to sing an old spiritual, "Free at Last," by J. W. Work, whose words inspired Martin Luther King's famous speech: "Free at last, free at last. I thank God I'm free at last."

On the morning they were to film that scene, Redd called together the extras and actors who were playing the mourners and announced that the words to the song had been changed. He taught them the new words. When Michael Anderson later shot the scene, much to his surprise they sang "Free at last, free at last. Abraham Lincoln has freed your a——."

CHAPTER TWELVE

Robert Hinkle, Producer

With a dog that kills snakes, herds cows, and catches fish, the story's easy.

—CHARLIE KING, PRODUCER OF *OLE REX*

The late 1950s into the 1960s were the golden days of television. It seemed like everybody was shooting a TV pilot and, before you knew it, they had a series. Why couldn't I do the same? I knew lots of people, and I'd done a lot of series work, so I knew who got things done and how they got them done. I'd already blown one shot at a big-time TV role by being friendly to Charles Marquis Warren, but my thoughts wandered to new opportunities. Besides, I had seen myself on the big screen as Frank James; maybe it was time to shift my focus to the small screen.

In 1959, I started looking for a good idea for a television pilot. The trick was to find something that hadn't been done yet, so that ruled out westerns, even though that was where I had the most expertise. I raised my sights skyward to a literal pilot.

I first met U.S. Air Force colonel Dean Hess through Rock Hudson. Recall that Rock was making a picture called *Battle Hymn* when George Stevens sent me over to talk to him that eventful day (for me at least) in 1955. *Battle Hymn* was based on a true story about an air force pilot who accidentally dropped a bomb on a German orphanage during World War II, killing a bunch of orphans. Overwhelmed with guilt, the pilot left the service to become a minister, then returned to the air force during the Korean War. There he helped organize what became known as Operation Kiddy Car Airlift, the rescue by air cargo planes of nearly a thousand Korean orphans from the advancing Chinese army. That pilot-turned-minister-turned-rescuer was Dean Hess.

Dean was now in charge of the U.S. Air Force Information Office in Los Angeles, which made him the official liaison between the air force and the motion picture industry. He had been technical adviser on *Battle Hymn* and technical supervisor on an earlier Korean War picture called *Dragonfly Squadron.* He and I became good friends. I'd even gone on a few jaunts with him to officers' and enlisted personnel's clubs. I'd take along some stuntmen and we'd stage fights for the military men and women, then Dean would talk about the picture business.

One day Dean and I were in my office at General Services Studio on Santa Monica Boulevard, talking about a possible series. "The air force has a plane called the X-13 that takes off and lands vertically," he said. "How about a show about the test pilots who fly those things? I can get you clearance to shoot at Edwards Air Force Base."

Now, that sounded pretty good. I could see some potential problems, though. I was already thinking like a producer. "That's kinda technical, isn't it?"

"Focus the stories on the people, the pilots. The planes are just props. I can get you cooperation through the Defense Department and all the stock footage from Ryan for any technical stuff you need."

Ryan Aeronautical Company, in San Diego, was the manufacturer of the plane officially known as the Ryan X-13A-RY Vertijet. As an interesting aside, T. Claude Ryan, the founder of predecessor Ryan Airlines Company, built the airplane Charles Lindbergh dubbed *The Spirit of St. Louis* and took on his famous 1927 transatlantic flight from New York to Paris.

I was intrigued by Dean's idea, so I ran it by George Stevens. George and I had remained friends since *Giant,* and I deeply respected his opinion. "It's got possibilities," he said, but I still wasn't sure. Test pilots aren't the same as combat pilots, and I figured most people had never heard of the X-13. This was one time where I put guts and BS on hold and moved cautiously. I didn't want to blow what might be my only shot at a TV series by making a show about something no one knew or cared about.

But former minister Dean kept preaching the idea, and he finally converted me. I would need three things to get started: a script, actors, and money. That was true in 1959 just as it is today. For the script I hired Vance Skarstedt, the writer of the crop-duster epic *No Place to Land.* He had written a few *Highway Patrol* episodes for television, so I knew he could write for the small screen.

For actors, I started with Dub Taylor. Dub already had a résumé as long as both my arms, and my pilot wouldn't even be the halfway mark in his long and illustrious career. In fact, he had over 230 credits, the last of which, before his death in 1994, was for Mel Gibson's *Maverick.*

Dub suggested John Agar for the lead. I didn't know John, but I knew his work, which included John Wayne pictures *Sands of Iwo Jima* and *She Wore a Yellow Ribbon.* I also knew that he'd had a drinking problem but that he'd been sober for a while, so I didn't think that would pose any problems.

I found a group of investors in Utah, including a fellow named Devon Standfield, to put up the money, and we were ready to go. True to his word, Dean got the footage from Ryan and arranged for us to shoot at Edwards, so in the summer of 1959 we shot a half-hour episode in black-and-white called *Test Pilot.* It cost only about twenty thousand dollars to

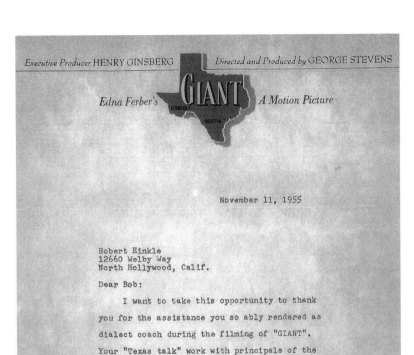

November 11, 1955

Robert Hinkle
12660 Welby Way
North Hollywood, Calif.

Dear Bob:

    I want to take this opportunity to thank
you for the assistance you so ably rendered as
dialect coach during the filming of "GIANT".
Your "Texas talk" work with principals of the
cast was an invaluable aid to greater realism,
and I am most appreciative.

                Sincerely,

                George Stevens

G
S
/
b
c

Letter to Bob from George Stevens about Bob's work on *Giant*.
Courtesy of Bob Hinkle.

Col. Dean Hess and Bob, *Test Pilot* (1959). Courtesy of Bob Hinkle.

make, which was cheap even for those days. I did most of the work myself, and I wasn't getting paid. I figured to make my money when we got a network deal. We no sooner had the pilot in the can when Pontiac made a semi-commitment to sponsor the show for NBC. It looked like I was on the verge of producing my first full-blown network television series on my very first try.

Then came another one of those unlucky moments that make life interesting. On New Year's Eve 1959, John Agar came to my house for a small get-together, then left for another party. He didn't drink at my house, but I guess he couldn't resist the temptation at his later stop. I picked up the paper the next morning to stare blankly at a headline announcing that he had been arrested for drunk driving. I suppose I should have been worried about John and his relapse, but I figured he was a big boy and could take care of himself.

My thoughts, selfishly, were only about what his arrest might do to our show.

Back then, drunk driving was sometimes swept under the rug or buried by publicists, but unfortunately for John, he was a repeat offender. To make matters worse, he had been driving with a suspended license. I told the investors to be prepared for the worst because it didn't seem likely that a car company such as Pontiac would want to sponsor a show featuring a serial drunk driver. Even an ol' west Texas cowboy could recognize the irony in that.

Sure enough, Pontiac backed out. Now I had to scramble to salvage what I could of the series. It was no longer a matter of how long the series would run and how rich and well-known I would become. Instead, now it was a question of how I could keep my investors from losing their money while at the same time trying to avoid a black mark against my name.

It's funny, sometimes, how luck can turn on a dime. At the same time we had been shooting *Test Pilot*, a guy named Al Simon was making an anthology series at General Services Studio, where we were working, called *Flight*. Air Force general George Kinney, a highly decorated World War II veteran, hosted the show for Simon, who later produced or executive produced some of the most successful television shows in history, such as *The Beverly Hillbillies, Mr. Ed, Petticoat Junction,* and *Green Acres*.

Not all of Simon's shows would be hits, though. Fortunately, *Flight* hadn't flopped yet—although it would—and since it was an anthology show, Simon needed content. We had run the completed *Test Pilot* episode several times at the studio's screening room, and the projectionist told Simon about it. With no more of an introduction than that, Simon offered to buy my episode for forty-six thousand dollars. I jumped on the offer like a chicken on a June bug. My share of the profit, after paying back my investors, kept me afloat financially until I could find my next producing project.

In 1961 I was visiting my friend Bob O'Donnell, who ran a movie distribution company in Dallas. He told me about an oil man in Wichita Falls named Charlie King who wanted to make a picture about this dog that was pretty well-known there. Movies about dogs always seem to touch a chord with families, so naturally I was interested. This was before *Savage Sam*, but *Lassie* and *Rin Tin Tin* were icons in the popular culture of the day, and *Old Yeller* had bled tear ducts bone dry all across America in 1957. As an aside, *Savage Sam* was actually a sequel to *Old Yeller*, and Sam was Yeller's son.

Bob put me in touch with Charlie, so I went to Wichita Falls to meet him. "Tell me about this dog," I said.

"He's this good-looking white spitz named Rex, and I've got footage of him that you're not gonna believe. He kills snakes, he works cattle, he even catches fish out of a pond. I think he'd be perfect for a family movie. It's the kind of thing Disney would do."

"You got a script?"

"No."

"You got a storyline?"

"With a dog that kills snakes, herds cow, and catches fish, the story's easy. And I've already got a camera and a cameraman who belongs to the union."

"What about money?"

"Don't worry about the money."

Music to my ears. By the time I got back to Los Angeles, I had a storyline in mind. Charlie was right: a story about a snake-killing, cattle-herding, fishing-in-a-pond dog would be easy to develop—just put a boy and the dog together, have them get lost or in trouble where the dog has to . . . well, let's see, kill snakes, herd cows, and catch fish, then the dad finds them both at the end, and you've got a movie called *Ole Rex*.

I had heard about this writer who had mostly written for television but was looking to move into directing. His name escapes me—I think his last name was Gielgud, though not the actor John—but maybe my mind is blocking the full name to protect me from a raft of bad memories. I outlined this very simple story for him, and we made a deal for about five thousand dollars for him to write and direct. That would turn out to be the worst, but maybe the most interesting, deal I ever made.

With the writer/director lined up, it was time to start casting. When you're working low budget, you usually go with friends and family, and this was no exception. I got my stuntman friend Whitey Hughes onboard.* He enlisted his brother Bill Hughes and Bill's son, Billy, or Little Bill. Bill Coontz, acting under the name William Foster, was going to play Billy's father. Billy would play the lead opposite Rex, and I would play the sheriff.

The actors and I caravanned to Wichita Falls from Los Angeles and arrived a few days early to make sure everything was set for the production. Things moved quickly and, before you knew it, we were ready to go. All we needed now was the script.

Yeah, about the script . . .

For starters, Gielgud missed his plane from Los Angeles to Dallas. He called and said he'd be there later and not to worry, but when you're ready to shoot a movie and everyone is waiting on the script and the director, you worry. Little did I know then that we might have been better off if he had never shown up.

When Gielgud finally arrived, I went to his hotel room to talk about the script. I asked Dick McCarty, a friend from Wichita Falls, and Whitey Hughes to come along in case I needed witnesses. I wasn't too happy with Gielgud for missing

---

*Whitey had a long career as a stuntman, including doing stunts in *Bill & Ted's Excellent Adventure.* Billy Hughes was just getting started in the business. He later had TV roles in shows such as *Leave It to Beaver, Dennis the Menace, Gunsmoke,* and *The Rifleman.* Bill Coontz had played roles in westerns such as *The Rebel, Wyatt Earp,* and *Rawhide.*

his plane and could have strangled him for little or nothing. I didn't want to do anything I'd regret later.

"Here's the story," Gielgud said. "You've got this kid who likes to peep in windows. Maybe his next-door neighbor is this good-looking woman, and he sneaks out at night and looks in."

I didn't like where this was going, but I figured I'd give him a chance to finish, just in case there was some unexpected twist, before I knocked him on his butt.

"One night she sees him at the window and calls the police. He takes off when the police get there and hides under a car. But there are rattlesnakes under the car. He tries to get out but gets caught under there; you know, maybe his coat or his belt gets hung on something. Now the snakes are about to get him, and that's when the dog saves him."

That was one of the stupidest stories I'd ever heard. The story I wanted was about a boy who finds a dog that had been bitten by a snake; even dogs need a backstory and motivation. The boy takes the dog home and nurses him back to health. The problem is that the boy's dad works in the oilfields, and he tells his son he has to get rid of the dog because in the next town they're going to, they have to live in a motel and can't keep a dog. So the boy and the dog run away, and the dad and his friends have to hunt for them. That's where the dog herds some cattle, catches some fish, then saves the boy when he falls into a pit full of rattlesnakes. After that, the dad is so happy that he lets his son keep the dog, and they all live happily ever after. Nothing fancy, nothing complex, nothing special, not going to win any Oscars—just a nice little family picture about a boy and his dog.

Instead, Gielgud had given me this Peeping Tom piece of crap that I wouldn't make for all the money in the world. I left his room in a near state of shock. I had a cast and crew ready to go, and I had no usable script. Dick, Whitey, and I went to the lobby to talk to Charlie and see if we could come up with any ideas on how to prevent an impending disaster. As we were sitting there, wondering how things could get any worse, I noticed a government-issue sedan pull up outside the hotel. Two guys in dark suits, white shirts, and ties got out and headed for the front door. Dick said, "Those guys are from the Wichita Falls FBI office."

They went to the front desk, then headed for Gielgud's room. I figured we were about to find out how the situation could get worse. In Hollywood, writers often talked to cops or the FBI to get technical advice on law enforcement issues. This SOB upstairs had a storyline about cops chasing a window peeper, and here he had called in the FBI to get technical advice. I couldn't imagine why he thought the FBI would concern itself with window peeping, but damned if it didn't appear as if that's what was going on.

A few minutes later, the two men came looking for me. "We're with the FBI," one of them said. Now he was supposed to say something like, "We can't offer technical advice on a movie like this. Just thought we'd let you know." Instead, he said, "We've got a warrant for the arrest of a fellow named Gielgud. He says he's working for you."

"You've got a what?" I asked.

"An arrest warrant."

"For what?"

"He was escorted off a plane in Los Angeles for saying he had a bomb."

Metal detectors and Homeland Security screenings may have ramped up since 9/11, but the authorities have always frowned on the idea of bombs on planes, even if mentioned in jest.

"Well," I said, "I suppose we better go up there and talk to this SOB."

Gielgud was livid. "Look," he said, "I never said I had a bomb. I was putting my briefcase in the overhead compartment, and the stewardess wouldn't let me because she said it might fall out and hurt someone. I simply told her that it had some sensitive instruments in it, and I thought it would be safer up there instead of under my seat. She didn't like that, so she made up something to get me thrown off the plane."

"That's not the way we heard it," one of the agents said. "Several witnesses confirm that you said what you had in there might blow up the plane."

That was pretty much the end of the discussion, and they hauled him off. As big a problem as we already had with the ridiculous screenplay he had written, now we had to figure out a way to get rid of him altogether. I called the Directors Guild of America, hoping they might offer a solution. Usually you have to pay a director after you've hired him or her, even if you fire the person, but I thought this case might be unusual enough to get a waiver. I didn't want Charlie to pay for a director he wasn't going to use, then have to pay again for his replacement. I explained my predicament, then held my breath.

"Bob," the guy from the guild said, "cut him loose and send him home. It would be a nice gesture to pay for his ticket, but you don't even have to do that."

That sounded pretty good to me. I told Charlie, who agreed that we should put Gielgud on the next plane. But when he got out on bond and I went to his room to give him the bad news, I found press people all over the place, with TV cameras rolling. The SOB had called a press conference to announce he was going to sue the airline for a million dollars. He even had gossip columnists like Hedda Hopper and Walter Winchell on the phone. I couldn't go busting in on the middle of his press conference, but I damn sure sent his butt home to California first thing the next morning. Problem solved.

Or was it?

There I was in Wichita Falls with actors, crew, and a cameraman, but no script and no director. I told Charlie, "I don't know what we can do except send everybody home and forget about it."

"Why don't you write the script and direct it?" he suggested.

"I've never directed anything before."

"Yeah, but you've seen it done a hundred times. And you stood next to George Stevens and watched him do it. Besides, you already know what the story is."

I was still reluctant, but Charlie added, "It's my money, and I'm willing to risk it."

If he was willing to risk his own money, who was I to say no? What followed next wasn't something they teach in film schools, but it was as good an education as you could hope for. Over the next few weeks I stayed up nights writing, then the following day we'd shoot what I had written. I had two secretaries helping out. I'd dictate to one, make changes to what she typed, then give it to number two to put into script form. I was treading water as fast as I could, ultimately trying to get about two days ahead of shooting. Sometimes we made it, sometimes we didn't.

Somehow it all worked out and, believe it or not, we ended up with a pretty good little picture about a boy and a snake-killing, cow-herding, pond-fishing dog named Rex. I took the finished product to Dallas and showed it to Bob O'Donnell, the man who had introduced me to Charlie King. As a movie distributor, I figured he had a pretty good feel for what would sell and what wouldn't. He was impressed enough to call his friend Hy Martin at Universal Pictures in New York and make an appointment for me.

Hy turned out to be a helluva nice guy, just as you'd expect for an ol' boy from Texas. He had worked in the film business in Dallas before going to Universal, so we had lots in common. We finally got around to talking about *Ole Rex*. "It's what, about forty-three-and-a-half minutes long?" he asked. "That means it's a featurette, not a full-blown feature."

Back in those days, when you went to the movies you usually got a two-picture deal: two features with a short subject in between that acted as a sort of intermission. What we had was too short to be a feature but too long to be a short subject in between two features. I could tell that I was about to get a "thanks, but no thanks." Then he surprised me.

"We're getting ready to release a picture by a young director named Stanley Kubrick, called *Spartacus*. It stars Kirk Douglas and Laurence Olivier." And it would get nominated for six Oscars and would win four. "We've been trying to decide what to do with it because it's really long. We don't think audiences will sit through two back-to-back features since the main event's so long. But a featurette leading into *Spartacus* is the perfect solution to our problem."

So Universal bought *Ole Rex* outright and released it nationally with *Spartacus*. My little picture ended up showing about 30 or 40 percent of the gross of *Spartacus*, since the box office was apportioned between the two movies, so it looked like it did a pretty good business. It didn't hurt my reputation any, either. It was another case of my being in the right place at the right time.

Looking back on it now, I can barely believe it. Charlie King, with whom I stayed close until the day he died, put his money where his mouth was; we ended up making the movie for about thirty-five thousand dollars, sold it for twice that, and got nationwide distribution with *Spartacus*. I don't know if it's because Charlie had faith in me or if it's because he had faith in Rex. I'm betting it was Rex.

One of the fun things that came out of *Ole Rex* was that it showed in my hometown of Brownfield, and Hiram Parker, the owner of the local theater, actually paid to fly me in for the premiere. I guess he had forgotten that in 1946 or 1947 he had banned R. J. Riley and me for life. Out of mischief, R.J. and I had taken a canister of black pepper into the balcony, then scattered the pepper on the folks below, just to hear them sneeze. I can't tell you why that seemed like fun at the time, but to a couple of teenagers it just did. We probably would have gotten away with it, too, if we hadn't run down the stairs and sprinted out of the lobby. I guess that was a pretty obvious sign of guilt. And then fifteen years or so later, all was apparently not only forgotten, but they were actually paying me to come back.

Another fun thing was going back to Wichita Falls with my family for the annual rodeo the spring after the movie was released. *Ole Rex* was a huge hit there, and the president of the rodeo, Dr. Ted Alexander, invited me to serve as grand marshal. The special guest was going to be Rex, who was supposed to kill snakes for a live audience. The first night he would kill one, the second night two, the third night three, and on the final night he'd kill four. It was going to be the damndest show anyone had ever seen.

Sure enough, a standing-room-only crowd showed up that first night. A local herpetologist had caught a bunch of big ol' rattlesnakes, which are plentiful in that part of the state, so the show was set. I wore my pistols and started out by doing some fast draws, then I talked a bit about the movie business and the making of *Ole Rex*. But as fascinating an attraction as I surely was, the crowd wasn't there to see or hear me.

When I finished, much to the audience's relief, the herpetologist came into the arena carrying a cage and a pole with a clamp at the end. Everybody knew what was in that cage, even if they couldn't see very well. I introduced him to the crowd, then he reached in with the clamp and drew out a five- or six-foot rattlesnake. That rattler was one ticked-off snake, I'll guarantee you that. He held the snake up to the microphone; the rattling filled the arena and probably went out to just about the whole town. The sound was enough to scare you to death.

Ol' Rex heard it and came to attention. You can talk about Pavlov's dogs all you want, but Rex was a prime example of what that was about. The hair on the back of his neck stood up. He bared his teeth; a low growl rumbled deep inside his throat. He looked around the arena, trying to locate the source of the sound.

Then the herpetologist dropped the snake on the dirt, and Rex made a beeline for it. He slid in on his hind feet and grabbed the snake behind the head. Then he went to running backward, head whipping back and forth to beat the band. The crowd went absolutely crazy. Before you knew it, Rex had snapped the head plumb off the snake. Its long body quivered, rattle still rattling, while the crowd clapped, hooted, and hollered. After a minute or two, the snake stopped moving. Game, set, and match to Rex.

Rex and the snake made the front page of the Wichita Falls newspaper the next day. That night it wasn't just standing room only; they broke all attendance records in the history of the rodeo. By the last night, the four-day record was also broken, even though there was bad weather in the area, right down to tornado warnings. It seemed like everybody wanted to see Rex kill four snakes. And he didn't disappoint.

The snake killing was right before the bull riding event, and that last night there were some mighty nervous cowboys. "Did he get all the snakes?" one of them asked me.

"All but one," I said. "But don't worry, we'll find it sooner or later."

If I hadn't broken down laughing, there might not have been any bull riding that night.

Dr. Alexander, the rodeo president, got calls from several other rodeos in the area asking to book Rex and me. Unfortunately, poor Rex got a tick in his ear, and while undergoing surgery to remove it, he died on the operating table.

I sure loved that ol' dog.

CHAPTER THIRTEEN

Making New Texans

*I'm getting ready to do a picture in Texas, and I'd like you to
work with me the way you did with James Dean on* Giant.
— PAUL NEWMAN

In April 1962, flush from my success with *Ole Rex*, the
cheers of the crowds at the Wichita Falls rodeo still ring-
ing in my ears, I wondered what I was going to do for an en-
core. A dog that kills rattlesnakes is a tough act to follow.
That's one of the downsides to a career in the movies: you're
only as good as your last picture. When you're on the rodeo
circuit, you always know where and when your next gig is.
Not so in Hollywood. With the wrap of each movie, you're
just an unemployed actor/director/producer/dialogue
coach/whatever on the hunt for your next project. And
when your specialty is Texas, you never know where that next
project is coming from.

For me, it came in the form of an unexpected telephone
call from an unlikely source. In those days, I had an answering
service in Los Angeles to take my calls lest I miss some new
opportunity. I checked with the service daily because I knew
that when directors or producers called, if they couldn't get
hold of you quickly they'd move down their lists to the next
name, so an answering service was a necessity. Their job was
simply to take a name and number for you; they weren't supposed to give your number to the caller. So I was shocked

when, as Sandy and I were packing to go back to Los Angeles from Wichita Falls, I received a call from someone who had gotten my number there from my answering service. My first thought was that I needed a new answering service.

My second thought was a bit more forgiving. The voice on the other end of the line sounded familiar; I just couldn't place it.

"Is this Bob Hinkle?"

"Yeah."

"This is Paul Newman."

My mind froze for a second. "Yeah, BS," I wanted to say. But damned if it didn't sure enough sound like Paul Newman. I had been a fan of his since he played the first Rocky in *Somebody Up There Likes Me*. And who could forget his Billy the Kid in director Arthur Penn's *The Left Handed Gun*? Even more recent was his Oscar-nominated portrayal of Fast Eddie Felson in *The Hustler*. Why the hell was Paul Newman calling me?

"I'm getting ready to do a picture in Texas, and I'd like you to work with me the way you did with James Dean on *Giant*. I'm playing a Texan, and I want to be a Texan on this picture. You up for that?"

Let's see, turn Fast Eddie Felson into a Texan? Well, he had played Billy the Kid, and New Mexico was just west of Texas. Why the hell not?

"Just tell me when and where you want to talk."

"Day after tomorrow, we're going to be in Amarillo. Can you meet me and the director and producer there?"

"That'd be fine. I'm in Wichita Falls right now, and that's not too far."

So we made a date to meet. Sandy and the kids and I stayed over another day in Wichita Falls, then meandered our way to Amarillo. There was no hurry because Paul and his producers weren't due until late afternoon, and I didn't want to hole up in a hotel room and just sit there watching the clock.

So en route we visited the 6666 Ranch in Guthrie, reputedly won in a poker game with a winning hand of four sixes (alas, not true), and the massive Pitchfork Ranch nearby, and we still arrived in Amarillo a couple of hours early.

My mind was awhirl with thoughts of my experiences on *Giant* and wondering how this new picture would compare. With Paul Newman attached, you knew it wasn't going to be a B picture. The question wasn't *whether* it would be big but *how* big it would be. I couldn't help but think that another lucky break had fallen into my lap for no reason other than I was a Texan.

A room was reserved for us at the Ramada Inn on the old Route 66, on the east side of Amarillo, so we checked in and waited, anticipation building.

"What do you think he'll say?" Sandy asked.

"Well, I think I've already got the job. It may just be a matter of whether I'll take it."

That was the optimist in me talking, or maybe it was just the cocky Texan. The way Paul had talked on the phone made it seem like a done deal, but you can never be sure until it actually happens.

"You are going to take it, aren't you?" she said. The sentence had a question mark at the end, but it came across as an exclamation point.

After what seemed like forever, the phone rang. I jumped up and snatched it.

"Hello?"

"Bob, this is Paul Newman. I've got Irving Ravetch and Marty Ritt in my room. Why don't you come over and get acquainted?"

I headed to Paul's room, wearing my standard Texas uniform—boots, starched jeans, western shirt, and big belt buckle. As I knocked on his door, I wasn't nervous. I had already worked with some of Hollywood's biggest stars. Still, your blood pressure kicks up a notch and your heart pumps a tick harder when you know you're about to confront opportunity. I've often heard it said that luck is what happens when preparation meets opportunity. Well, I'd spent my entire life preparing for opportunities just like this. Luck was becoming a fairly constant companion.

After a few seconds the door opened, and I stood face-to-face with Paul Newman.

"Hi, Bob," he said as he extended his hand. "Come on in."

He introduced me to Marty and Irving, both of whom were casually dressed. Marty even had on a pair of coveralls, already feeling at home in west Texas. We sat around a small coffee table and shot the breeze for a while. There was a script on the table, and I thumbed through it as we talked. They outlined exactly what they wanted and needed from me: to turn the cast into a group of walking, talking Texans. I felt a sense of déjà vu: I'd had a nearly identical conversation years earlier in George Stevens's office.

They also made it clear that they didn't want me to be merely another member of the crew. "We want you intimately involved in everything," Marty said. "We want you on the set every day, right there with us. Consider yourself part of the executive team."

They kept that promise in every detail, right down to having a chair on the set for me next to Paul's. When people treat you with that kind of respect and make you feel appreciated, it makes you want to work that much harder for them. I wanted to help make their movie the best damn picture about Texas ever made. Even better than *Giant*. I don't know if that was part of their calculation or if they were just nice folks, but either way, it paid off for all of us.

After about an hour, we wrapped things up. They arranged for someone to babysit my kids, then graciously took Sandy and me to dinner. The next morning I packed my family into the car and sent them off to Los Angeles, and I went to work.

Martin Ritt and Irving Ravetch made quite a team in Hollywood, and they would continue to do so for a lot of years after *Hud*. They had worked together, and with Paul, on *The Long, Hot Summer* in 1958, and the trio would work together again on *Hombre* in 1967. Marty and Irving would also work together without Paul several times over the next few decades.*

Hud is an adaptation of a novel by Texas's own Larry McMurtry, best known (later) for *Lonesome Dove*. Irving had been traveling between the East Coast and Los Angeles when he stopped in Dallas, where he picked up a copy of McMurtry's *Horseman, Pass By*. He had read it by the time he got to Los Angeles, where his first call was to Marty Ritt. They had just finished working on *The Long, Hot Summer* and were looking for another project. "I've got Paul's next movie," he said.

It took a while for them to track down and get the rights from McMurtry, who was then just an obscure Texas novelist. Irving and his writing partner from *The Long, Hot Summer*, Harriett Frank, Jr. (who was also his wife), adapted the novel, and Irving and Marty struck a deal at Paramount. In the spring of 1962, they were ready to go to west Texas.

The movie was going to be shot near the town of Claude, a mere speck of dust on the horizon about thirty miles east of Amarillo. We spent the first week in Amarillo working with the script and rehearsing, usually in Paul's room at the Ramada Inn. We had a kitchen table set up, and the cast and I would sit with Marty and Irving and read through the script, over and over. We made some minor story changes based on my suggestions, and it made me feel good to know that my contributions were recognized.

---

*Including *Norma Rae*, with Sally Field (1979); *Murphy's Romance*, with James Garner and Sally Field (1985); and *Stanley and Iris*, with Robert DeNiro and Jane Fonda (1990).

As with *Giant*, I found myself overwhelmed by the quality of the cast, all of whom had descended on west Texas for the filming. Patricia Neal, who would win an Oscar for best actress in a supporting role for *Hud*, had spent much of her career up 'til then in television, including such notables as *Studio One* and *Playhouse 90*. She had been acting since 1949, when she appeared in *The Fountainhead*, and was fresh off her performance with Audrey Hepburn in *Breakfast at Tiffany's*. Patricia was nominated for a second Oscar in 1969, this time for best actress in a leading role, for *The Subject Was Roses*, with Jack Albertson and Martin Sheen. In *Hud* she played Alma, the housekeeper who tries to keep the Bannon family in line and the ne'er-do-well Hud at arm's length.

Patricia was extremely nice to me throughout the filming. In some ways she reminded me of Mercedes McCambridge, who played Luz Benedict in *Giant*. She caught on fast to Texan-speak, which isn't easy to do. Popular culture has its own stereotype about what Texans sound like, but it takes a real actor to get the nuances of the speech down like Patricia did.

The head of the Bannon family was played by Melvyn Douglas, who would win an Oscar for best actor in a supporting role for *Hud*, would be nominated for best actor in a lead role for *I Never Sang for My Father* in 1971, and would win another supporting Oscar for *Being There*, with Peter Sellers, in 1980.

I explained to Melvyn that the trick to being a Texan was slowing everything down. "You know, these old Texas ranchers don't get in a hurry about anything," I said. "They've been in a hurry all their lives, and now, in their later years, they're ready to take things easy." You had to tell him only once, and he'd work until he'd mastered it. Like Jimmy, the only thing he couldn't do was chew tobacco. I tried to teach him, but he gave it up pretty quick. By the time we were ready to shoot, he could have doubled for any number of actual ranchers I knew in west Texas.

Bob, Patricia Neal, and an unidentified woman, on the set of *Hud* (1962). Courtesy of Bob Hinkle.

Rounding out the cast, in addition to Paul, was Brandon DeWilde. No western aficionado can forget the young Brandon calling after Alan Ladd in the closing scene of *Shane*, a role for which Brandon was nominated for a supporting actor Oscar in 1954. He was the only major actor not nominated for an Academy Award in *Hud*, but he accepted Douglas's Oscar at the awards ceremony since Melvyn was in Israel at the time.

Brandon was a little overweight when the filming started, but he went on a strict diet and lost about twenty pounds during the shoot. If you watch the movie closely, you can see the difference. He was very disciplined and easy to work with. I think Brandon had as much or even more talent than anyone in the cast. His career was tragically cut short in a manner reminiscent of Jimmy Dean—he was killed in a car accident in July 1972 at age thirty while on his way to perform in a stage presentation of *Butterflies Are Free*.

I really appreciated the fact that all these talented actors treated me as if I actually had something to offer. For the most part, they followed what I said without question, and if they didn't, they'd explain why rather than just ignore me. With talent like that surrounding me, from actors to director to cinematographer James Wong Howe, who would also win an Oscar for *Hud*, I found myself again, as with *Giant*, sittin' in tall cotton indeed.

While rehearsing in Amarillo, we had to make some pretty severe changes to the screenplay dialogue. Irving Ravetch and Harriett Frank, Jr., were wonderful screenwriters, but they weren't Texans. Their version of McMurtry's Bannons came off like a Yankee family. But the Bannons were not only Texans, they were west Texans. We also couldn't have them sounding like city folk from Houston or Dallas, who were as foreign on the dusty plains as if they had stepped off a plane from New England. So Irving, Harriett, the cast, and I spent a lot of time putting the right flavor into the words.

I also had a pointer or two for the actors on things besides speech. For instance, with Paul's character, Hud Bannon, I explained that he would wear neat jeans with a crease in them, a starched shirt, and a hat that wasn't bent up in the back. A Texan, especially from one of the big ranches, would take pride in his appearance rather than show up dirty and dusty with an old beat-up hat, like some in Hollywood might assume. It was my job to make sure that if they wanted to walk, talk, act, and look like real Texans, they did in fact *walk*, *talk*, *act*, and *look* like real Texans instead of like something from a comic book or a dime novel.

Even after rehearsals ended and shooting started, I continued to spend a lot of time with Irving and Harriett on the script. They picked my brain constantly, trying to stuff as much real Texas as possible—and not just dialogue—into their limited cultural background. I suppose they might not consider their cultural backgrounds limited, but I feel like you're not really cultured unless you've first been truly steeped in the world of Texans. I consider my contributions on films like *Hud* and *Giant* as simply doing my small part for world culture.

In Amarillo, Paul and I discovered go-kart racing at a track a mile or so from our hotel. We quickly developed into fierce competitors. Brandon went with us a few times, and one of the assistant directors went a time or two, but this was really something between Paul and me. I loved it—the speed and the danger reminded me a little of my rodeoing days—but Paul really got hooked, just as Jimmy had on rabbit hunting.

We rarely wore helmets, and everybody recognized Paul Newman. After a while, word got out that he was a regular, and a crowd of spectators usually gathered when we raced. Paul was good about posing for pictures with folks, and I had my share of pictures taken as well. They didn't know who I was, but if I was with Paul Newman they figured I must have been somebody. The track owner probably had an uptick in his business because we were out there so often. I suppose it's a little late to ask for a commission.

I don't know if this was the genesis of Paul's interest in car racing, but we started going a couple of times a week. The rest of the crew was a little worried that we spent so much time there, and the suits were real worried. What if something happened to Paul? If their star was injured, it would put the whole production in jeopardy.

One night, Irving and Marty came out to watch. Paul and I were neck and neck on the track, the crowd cheering us on.

Marty Ritt and Bob, on the set of *Hud* (1962). Courtesy of Bob Hinkle.

Paul nosed ahead just as we rounded a corner. His kart swung a little wide, a tire clipped a bale of hay that formed the barrier, and next thing I knew he was flying upside down. The kart slammed down on the roll bar, so there was no real danger, but it was enough to scare the hell out of all of us. I jumped out of my kart and ran over to him.

Paul was hanging upside down. I grabbed the front of the cart and, using all my strength, flipped it over on its wheels. Paul's head wobbled as the kart slammed down, its motor still running. "God, let him be okay," I prayed.

"You all right?" I asked, trying to keep the worried tone out of my voice.

He smiled, nodded . . . and floored it. The little go-kart roared off, leaving me to hustle back to my kart and try to catch up. Afterward, Marty said, "I think maybe you and Paul need to cut down on the racing." He didn't say quit; he just said "cut down." We stopped going so often, but we still went every couple of weeks or so. There was no way Paul was going to stop altogether. When I say he was hooked, I mean he was hooked.

Claude, the county seat of Armstrong County, was named after a Fort Worth & Denver train engineer. In the late 1800s it was little more than a water stop for the train. One day the engineer looked out at the hotel while his train took on water. He stopped a passing cowboy. "What's the name of this town?"

"Doesn't have one. The town fathers keep haggling over it, but they can't agree."

"Why don't you name it for me? Name's Claude Ayers."

"I'll pass it along," the cowboy said. He did, and the powers that be agreed on Claude as a compromise. Claude Ayers never lived there, but he's buried in the Claude graveyard a few blocks off U.S. Highway 287, which runs from Dallas–Fort Worth to Amarillo and beyond.

The town has a nice courthouse square downtown, with the train track nearby, perfect for what we needed. The producers of *Hud* weren't the first to recognize Claude's value as a set. Director Fred Zinneman had filmed *The Sundowners* there in 1960, starring Deborah Kerr and Robert Mitchum. In 1977 it would be the site of *Sunshine Christmas*, starring Cliff DeYoung.

Hud is the story of a west Texas rancher trying to hold his ranch together in spite of the best efforts of his rebellious son, Hud, to take control. As if that weren't enough, his herd is wiped out by an epidemic of hoof-and-mouth disease, putting him on a head-on collision course with Hud. Paul's character is a first-class jerk—a boozing, womanizing, brawling young man with no respect for his father. He secretly harbors guilt over the death of his brother years earlier, leaving him to serve as a poor substitute of a father figure for his nephew Lonnie, played by Brandon. What better location for *Hud*, a movie about a cattle ranch, than Claude, which grew up as a cattle-shipping town in the late 1800s?

Just like the citizens of Marfa on *Giant*, the fine people of Claude took good care of us. We had to rely on lots of things from Amarillo, such as catering, because Claude, with a population of under a thousand, was too small to offer everything we needed, but you couldn't ask for better hosts. That may have surprised the folks from Los Angeles, but not me. After all, I knew—and still know—that the people in west Texas are the best people anywhere on this earth. It's truly God's country.

We ate well on the set. Barbecue was a favorite, and I made sure we got the best barbecue Amarillo had to offer. That wasn't without its dangers, though. One time I had the caterer bring in a supply of pork ribs. Who wouldn't like a nice big plate of pork ribs, I thought? Well, the folks who wouldn't like it were the Jewish folks, like Marty Ritt and Irving Ravetch. That settled that: from then on, I ordered brisket.

As we got into filming, I sat next to Marty, right by the camera. After each scene was shot, he'd ask, "What did you think of that, Bob?"

I'd put in my two cents as to how Texas it was, and we'd either reshoot the scene or move on to the next. At night I'd watch the rushes with Marty and Irving, and they'd want to know what I thought. I never critiqued the acting; who was I to criticize the likes of Paul Newman, Melvyn Douglas, and Patricia Neal? The highest compliment I could ever pay was, "It's sure looking like a Texas story to me."

They shot the film in black and white, which I didn't understand at first. I wasn't sure the movie-going public wanted to retreat from color. There's not a lot of color in that part of

Texas, though, so maybe it created the right mood. It also seemed to fit the tone of the story, which is depressing and drab, and cinematographer James Wong Howe was the best in the business at black and white. Later, after I saw the completed film, it never occurred to me that it should have been shot in anything other than black and white.

I couldn't wait to go to work each day. They paid me well but, hell, I'd have done this movie for nothing just for the chance to associate with these folks. I didn't tell them that, of course, because I needed money as much as the next guy. Like a lot of wives, Sandy enjoyed nice things, and she had discovered the difference between gold and sterling silver a long time ago. If I'd been single, though, I would have worked on this one for a lot less.

Paul's character was a big drinker. The script called for him to drink Four Roses Bourbon, and that just wouldn't do. Too highfalutin. "A Texan would drink Black Label Jack Daniels," I told Paul and Marty Ritt.

"Do you think you can get us some empty bottles?" Marty asked. They didn't want the actual whiskey, just the bottles. Then they'd concoct a mixture of Coca-Cola and water until it was the color of whiskey and fill the bottles with it.

I contacted Lone Star Distributors in Amarillo, the local Jack Daniels distributor, and they put me in touch with the Motlow family in Lynchburg, Tennessee, who owned the Jack Daniels distillery there. "I'm working on a movie in west Texas," I told them, "and I was wondering if I could get some empty half-pint bottles of Jack Daniels." Then I added the kicker: "It's for Paul Newman."

That was the magic key that opened all doors. "How many do you need?"

Next thing you know, the distributor showed up on the set with three cases of empty Jack Daniels bottles. He also included four or five cases of Lone Star beer, which I kept in a cooler in my room. I had noticed that Paul was a big beer drinker, with Coors his beer of choice. As part of transforming him into a Texan, I felt it was my duty to introduce him to Texas's own Lone Star beer. Sometimes when we'd rehearse at night, Paul would want to go to my room. "The beer's a little colder over there," he'd say. So we'd pop open two or three Lone Stars and rehearse his lines.

We got to be really good buddies during this time, much as I had with Jimmy Dean, though not as close. Paul had known Jimmy, but not well, so I'd tell him stories about working on *Giant*. We also talked about our families. I met his wife, Joanne Woodward, who came to Texas every two or three weeks. She would always give me a big hug and a kiss and thank me for working with Paul. Paul and Joanne didn't live far from Universal Studios, and after we got back to Los Angeles, Sandy and I saw them from time to time. It seemed like he had a party or something nearly every weekend, and he'd invite us over. I had many a good meal at the Newman/Woodward house.

We were there one time at a swimming party, and their housekeeper baked a vanilla cake with chocolate icing that was one of the best things I've ever put in my mouth. I insisted on getting the recipe, and we use it to this day—we call it the "Paul Newman Cake." I can't tell you how many times I've eaten it over the years, probably a lot more than Paul did. You just had to look at the two of us to know that I'm definitely better fed than he was.

Like I said, Paul and I became good buddies, but those late night conversations picked at the scab that had formed on my heart after Jimmy died. Jimmy and I spent more time together, and we planned our futures together. Over a relatively short period of time, we had become as close as brothers. As much as I loved working with Paul, there would never be another James Dean.

CHAPTER FOURTEEN

Do I Get Credit
for Those Oscars?

Boy, this is the worst piece of s—— I have ever seen.
—PARAMOUNT STUDIO EXECUTIVE

One day, Elvis Presley and his entourage passed through Amarillo on their way from Los Angeles to Memphis. I first met Elvis in 1956 in Shreveport, Louisiana. Elvis's promoter, Colonel Tom Parker, called Chill Wills and told him about this young guy Parker wanted Chill to put under contract. Chill and I flew to Shreveport to watch Elvis perform on the Louisiana Hayride. We knew Elvis was on his way to the big-time when Hank Snow, who followed Elvis, came off the stage complaining, "That kid will never be on another one of my shows."

Hank had been a regular at the Grand Ole Opry for a couple of years, using Elvis as his opening act, and he co-managed Elvis with Colonel Parker for a while. But by the time Elvis finished draining the audience at the Louisiana Hayride, there wasn't a handclap left for Hank. It was the damndest thing I ever saw, and jealousy got the better of Hank's business sense.

Later, when Elvis came to Hollywood to get into the picture business, Colonel Parker lived in Chill's guesthouse for a couple of months while Elvis rented a place in Brentwood.

I got to know Elvis pretty well during that time, along with Red West and Charlie Hodge, who made up part of his entourage.*

Anyway, as Elvis and his entourage passed through Amarillo, Red said to Elvis, "Ol' Hinkle's working on that movie with Paul Newman here."

"Let's stop by and say hello," Elvis said. "I'd like to meet Paul Newman."

They stopped at the Ramada Inn, where Elvis went inside to speak to an awestruck hotel clerk. "Is Bob Hinkle here?"

"He's on the set in Claude. They don't usually get back until about six or so."

"I can't wait that long. Be sure and tell him I said 'hi.'"

Then they left. The local news people found out, and when we got back to the hotel that evening, everybody wanted to know what in the hell Elvis Presley had been doing in Amarillo looking for Bob Hinkle.

Making movies is all about staying under budget—or at least *on* budget—and as is often the case, that's about staying on schedule. When you get behind, you start doing things that cost more money, like working longer days and doing night shoots, or you do things that hurt the integrity of the film, like cutting scenes or doing fewer takes. Or you move off location, back to the studio, and lose the character of the film's setting.

We weren't too far into filming on *Hud* when we fell a week to ten days behind schedule. That's not uncommon in filmmaking, especially when you're shooting on location, as we were. The book the script was based on was complex, and

---

*Red was in a number of Elvis's pictures, usually in uncredited roles, including *Blue Hawaii*, *Kid Galahad*, *Viva Las Vegas*, and *Girls! Girls! Girls!* Later he worked in television, appearing in such series as *The Wild Wild West* and *Baa Baa Blacksheep*. Charlie also had some uncredited roles in movies such as *Clambake*, *Speedway*, and *Charro*.

the characters were similarly complex, and some of the scenes turned out to be more complicated than anyone thought during preproduction. Marty made the actors rehearse more and he shot more takes, which pushed things behind. Surprisingly, Paramount didn't seem concerned. We didn't find out until much later that the executives weren't thrilled about a black-and-white movie with Paul Newman playing such a jerk. I guess they thought if we got far enough behind, we'd never finish. They'd just write it off on their income tax, then move on to pictures with happier endings. I knew we were making a great movie, though, and I was a part of it. That was all I cared about.

Somebody dubbed my hotel room "Bob's Tavern" because of the neon Lone Star beer sign on my wall that I had gotten from the local distributor. I had also swapped some of those boxes of Jack Daniels for a variety of types of booze at a liquor store across the street, and my room became a popular gathering place. It originally had two double beds, but I asked the hotel to replace one with a couch and a couple of good-sized chairs to accommodate my patrons.

One evening, Marty and Irving came calling at Bob's Tavern. I ushered them in and, like a hospitable bartender, asked, "What'll you have?"

"Beer," they both said. They, too, had learned to be good Texans.

I fetched Lone Stars from the cooler and passed them out. They sat in chairs while I resumed my reclining position on the bed.

"Bob, we've got a problem," Irving said. "You know that softball scene?"

I knew the one he was talking about. It was where a bunch of ranchers and town folks played a Kiwanis Club softball game. In the bottom of the last inning, Hud is supposed to come to bat, with his team behind, and hit the game-winning homerun. Now, I know that's been done a hundred times before. But it was an important scene because it set the stage for a bit of reconciliation between Hud and his father.

"We're behind schedule, and Paramount is finally starting to get on us about the cost," Marty said. "They want us back in California, so we need to replace that scene with something we can shoot when we get there." He took a long sip of his Lone Star. "Got any ideas?"

That was one of my biggest roles on the picture: coming up with ideas. They often consulted me on wardrobe matters to make sure we stayed true to Texas, and sometimes I was asked to do more than simply consult with the writers by actually rewriting a line or two of dialogue. They were astute enough to realize that a screenwriter from anywhere other than Texas had a tendency to write dialogue for Texans that sounded the way folks from the East or the South might talk, or it might slip into a cartoonish stereotype. My job was to keep a watchful eye out for things like that.

One time, for example, they asked me if I knew who Albert Schweitzer was. It seems the script was making some political point, and it mentioned Schweitzer in dialogue. I had no idea who he was and told them so, and they ended up cutting that line. I guess they thought if I didn't know who he was, then none of the other Texas hicks would know either, so the point would be wasted on much of the audience.

I had already been thinking about that softball scene because I didn't think it worked, but I hadn't said anything. When your advice is sought, it's more welcome than when it's pushed.

"Do a pig scramble," I said.

"A what?" they both responded at once. Ahhh, the frustrations of dealing with non-Texans.

"Every self-respecting ranch kid has been involved in a pig scramble at a rodeo or a fair. Get ten or fifteen pigs and grease 'em up real good with lard. Then bring all the kids out of the stands and turn those pigs loose. The first kid to catch one and bring it to the announcer's stand wins a prize. Only instead of doing it with kids, we'll do it with grown men, like Hud. When we get back to Los Angeles, I can get some stuntmen to help out."

"That's a great idea," Marty said. You could tell that he and Irving were already starting to play the scene in the theaters of their minds. It was pure Texas. "That'll look great on film."

"Tell you what," Irving said, "put it down on paper and let me take a look at it. If it works, we might even give you part credit for the screenplay." We had a good laugh at that one. Screenwriters don't give away part of their credit to anyone without a fight.

After they left, I went to the production office and borrowed a typewriter, then banged out a pig scramble scene. There was some dialogue in the original scene that we needed to keep. As I mentioned, the purpose of the scene was to get Hud back in his father's good graces, and the lines spoken among Patricia Neal, Brandon DeWilde, and Melvyn Douglas while they were in the stands watching were important. My job was to keep the dialogue but to layer it into a visual of a pig scramble instead of a softball game. I also came up with some lines of my own that I thought would fit the new scenario.

I stayed up late, but it wasn't my first time working all night on a script. Remember *Ole Rex*? After something like that, this was a breeze. I gave my pages to Marty and Irving first thing the next day. They took a quick look while I waited for the verdict. "That's perfect," Marty said. "We'll shoot it just like you wrote it."

Back in Los Angeles, I rounded up a group of my stunt buddies, then located a guy who raised pigs and got him to bring a bunch to Pickwick Stables on Riverside Drive in Burbank, where they do horse shows. They had a nice riding ring where we could rehearse, but we did the actual shoot at a place near the edge of Glendale and Burbank. Pickwick was way too nice to double as a small-town rodeo arena, but it was perfect for our rehearsal.

We spent close to an hour chasing the pigs, falling all over each other in the process, but we figured out some pretty good stunts and gags that I thought would be perfect for the scene. I think it was similar to choreographing a Broadway dance number, but I suspect most dancers would be insulted by the comparison.

The day we shot the scene, Marty wanted us to go through it one more time first. "You play the announcer," he told me. "And since you wrote this scene, you direct it. When it's ready to rehearse, let me know so I can come watch. In the meantime, I'll be listening to the Dodgers on the radio."

With that, he walked off and left me in charge.

In charge!

I could hardly believe it. I'd done bit parts and stunt work, and I'd directed one little ol' picture—not even a full-blown feature but a featurette—and now I was going to be directing the likes of Paul Newman, Patricia Neal, Melvyn Douglas, and Brandon DeWilde, with Academy Award–winning cinematographer James Wong Howe under my command. On top of all that, I was going to have my stunt buddies taking orders from me. They'd be punching each other and saying, "Look at ol' Hinkle; that SOB is in charge of this whole damn thing."

I was sweating it on the inside, but I faked it on the outside, cool as a cucumber. We set up the scene, then I sent the assistant director to fetch Marty. When he got back, we ran through it while he watched. "Looks good to me, Bob," he said. "Let's do it."

We got everybody into position, and I yelled "roll 'em!" I was showing off, but it still felt good. It took about three hours to get everything just right because this was a major production, with lots of camera setups, close-ups, and long shots. I was giving orders and moving people around. I felt as if I had been born to do this.

The scene came out just fine, if I do say so myself, but you can watch the movie and judge for yourself.

I had a chance to give some of my buddies more work in a barroom brawl scene. Stuntmen live for barroom brawls! In the scene, there's a guy in the bar giving Lonnie, played by Brandon, a hard time, and Hud comes to his rescue. Hud liked a good fight, so coming to Lonnie's defense was a fringe benefit for him. The way Marty and the stunt coordinator set it up, Hud was supposed to start sparring with this jerk who was hassling Lonnie. They had him dancing around like it was a boxing match, not a bar fight. That may be the way guys fight in some places, but Texans do things differently.

"Hud's not going to do that," I told Marty. "He's going to want to end it before it barely gets started."

"I don't understand what you're saying."

"Let me show you." I turned to Paul. "Put your hand up on that post where it's in position to get a good shot at him. What you're going to do is swing your fist off that post and knock him out with just one lick."

Marty got everybody in position, and we shot it the way I suggested. Hud knocks that ol' boy out with one punch, then everybody else gets in on the action. It's a grand barroom brawl. My stunt buddies made a couple of hundred dollars apiece off that scene, and that thrilled them.

We finished the movie in about five months, at a total production cost in the neighborhood of $6 million. I don't know what that translates to in today's dollars, but that was a pretty nice neighborhood in 1962. The studio executives still weren't too excited about the picture, and they did everything they could to delay its release. The first debate was over what to call it. They discussed using the novel's title, *Horseman, Pass*

By, but discarded that idea. Then they decided on *Hud Bannon,* but that didn't have any ring to it—no pizzazz.

Finally, I said, "Everybody's going to be talking about what Paul's character does in the movie. It'll be 'Hud did this' and 'Hud did that.' One-name titles always seem to work, like *Shane* or *Giant.* Why don't you just call it *Hud?*"

I don't know if it was simply at my suggestion or if someone else had the same idea, but I do know that they put *Hud* on the first print, and it stuck.

The next issue arose during a private screening for Paramount executives. None of the cast would be there because the execs wanted to talk freely, and they might not be honest if they knew Marty or Irving or Paul was listening. The production team was incredibly nervous. They had put months of their lives into the picture, and now a bunch of businessmen who hadn't been on the set were going to pass judgment. Their reaction could determine how much the studio would push the movie when it was released or whether they would even release it at all. Whatever they decided, careers were on the line.

On the day of the screening, Marty pulled me aside. "Bob, go over there and watch it with them. I want to know what they say."

"They won't let me in."

"Just ease in after it gets started and then ease out at the end so no one notices you. They'll think you're one of the technicians."

I was as interested as anybody to find out what the big shots thought, but I had a career at stake, too, so I sure didn't want to get caught. That evening I went into the projection room while the projectionist got the picture ready, as if I were a technician. Once the movie started, I slipped into the screening room and took a seat at the back. Marty was right; no one paid attention to me.

When the movie was over and the lights came up, there was silence for a moment. I held my breath. I thought it looked pretty damn good, but I knew my opinion didn't count. Then one of the execs, I believe it was a guy from New York, piped up. "Boy, this is the worst piece of s—— I have ever seen. Who wants to see a black-and-white movie anymore? And man, it's depressing. Makes me want to slit my wrists."

"Women are going to hate Paul Newman," someone else said.

They groused for a while longer, but the trend had been set. When I left the screening room, I faced the longest walk of my life. What was I gonna say when I got to Marty's office? I didn't want to outright lie, but I couldn't tell the unvarnished truth either. These folks had become my friends, and I didn't want to hurt their feelings. I put my brain into high gear, trying to come up with the right way to deliver the bad news.

Marty was waiting for me, along with Paul, Irving, and Harriett.

"What the hell did they say?" Marty asked.

"Well, some of them weren't too happy because it was in black and white."

"Yeah," Marty said, "we expected that. What else did they say?"

"Well, they're worried how women are going to take to the character of Hud. That's not the Paul Newman they're used to."

I was mindful of the adage about shooting the messenger, but everyone could tell from my reluctance that the news wasn't good. Fortunately, Paramount had too much money in the movie to scrap it, so they held a sneak preview in Encino to gauge the public's reaction. Each audience member was given a card to fill out; at the end of the movie, the results were tabulated. To the studio's surprise, it was nearly unanimous: all "excellents" and "superbs." Some studio honcho figured, in the way only honchos can, that the results meant only one thing: the cast and crew had sneaked in friends and family to skew the survey. So they held another sneak preview

Paul Newman (1962). Courtesy of Bob Hinkle.

in San Diego. This time they didn't let anyone know about it until it was over.

And guess what? Same result.

Based on that, the studio decided to hold its nose and release the picture in 1963. Lo and behold, not only did it find an avid audience, it ended up winning three Oscars: best actor in a supporting role, Melvyn Douglas; best actress in a leading role, Patricia Neal; and best cinematography, black and white, James Wong Howe. In addition, it was nominated for four more Academy Awards: best actor in a leading role, Paul Newman; best art direction—set direction, black and white; best director, Martin Ritt; and best writing, screenplay based on material from another medium, Irving Ravetch and Harriet Frank, Jr. Bill Cosby even paid tribute to it with a routine called "Hoof and Mouth" on his *Bill Cosby Is a Very Funny Fellow, Right?* album.

Paul was on the outs with the Academy because he thought the awards were based on the good ol' boy system, pitting actors against each other, and he had gone public with his criticisms. He should have won that year, but there was no way he was going to after expressing that sentiment, which sorta proved his point.

One of the fun things about writing your memoir is reminiscing about things you've done in your life and the wonderful people you've met along the way. One of the worst parts about it, though, is losing some of those people. Paul and I stayed in touch over the years, sometimes talking on the phone or simply exchanging birthday or Christmas cards. I called Paul a few months before he died, but he was out. I spoke for a while with Joanne Woodward, who told me he wasn't doing that well. "I don't know how much longer we're going to have him," she said.

And then we lost him on September 26, 2008. I'm richer for having known him.

CHAPTER FIFTEEN

Life Is Good

I don't know about you boys, but I got to take a leak.
—Lyndon Johnson, president of the United States

One of the quirky things about the movie business is that you can't accurately plot your course. Your only real choice is whether to go into the business in the first place, but once you do, if you stick with it you bounce around like a pinball. Job security is a foreign concept. When you're working in the movies, as opposed to television, every time you finish a picture you're unemployed again until you find the next one. In television, you're only secure until your series gets canceled, which can happen any day. Talent is good, but luck is better. More often than not, it's about being in the right place at the right time. And you never know where or when that is.

It was 1962. *Hud* was finished, and I was looking for a job. Out of the blue, a buddy named Paul Wolf called me with a proposition. Paul ran the photography department at Saint Joseph Hospital in Burbank, and he had been approached by several doctors about producing instructional training movies on medical procedures. It sounded interesting and was at least tangentially related to movies. I had nothing better to do, so I said yes.

Paul and I teamed with Bob Dicus, who was in charge of the hospital's physical therapy department, and formed Cinema Pictures, Inc. Pretty soon, what had started as a lark turned into a full-time job. We produced about three films a month, on procedures ranging from facelifts (very popular in Hollywood then, as they are now) to hair transplants to cleft palate surgery. Rather than just create documentary-type films, I wrote scripts with storylines and characters that involved the medical procedures. I figured we might as well entertain as well as educate. We ultimately made about forty or fifty films, which earned us a pretty good income over the next few years.

One of the most successful was called *Dr. Heart*, about Saint Joseph's cardiac crisis team. Anytime you heard something like "Dr. Heart, please report to room three-twelve" on the hospital public address system, you knew the crisis team had been called into action. I used Bill Coontz, my buddy from *Ole Rex*, to play a patient already in the hospital who suffers a heart attack—something that happens more often than you might think. Then we see the cardiac crisis team in action. I got Rock Hudson to narrate, and *Dr. Heart* showed in virtually every Catholic hospital in the country.

My biggest regret on *Dr. Heart* is that I wasn't able to foresee how popular "blooper" outtakes would become. In the script, Bill suffers his heart attack and blacks out, then this beautiful blonde nurse brings him back with mouth-to-mouth resuscitation. When we got ready to film, I paid one of the cleaning staff—a seriously overweight woman with a good sense of humor—to substitute for the blonde without Bill knowing it.

"Don't roll cameras," I told the cameraman. "No need to waste film on a joke."

As we started the scene, Bill had a beautiful heart attack—cinematically speaking, of course. Our stand-in leaned over to begin mouth-to-mouth. Just at that moment, Bill opened his eyes. I guess he wanted the full experience of being resuscitated by a beautiful blonde. But when he saw a different, much larger face coming his way—well, let's just say he did a pretty good Lazarus impression rising up out of that bed. Looking back with twenty-twenty hindsight, I'd have damn sure had cameras rolling; we'd have been on every blooper show on television, maybe even in the blooper hall of fame.

One day a fan of *Ole Rex* named Leonard Stevens, a professional hunter who specialized in capturing wild animals for zoos and circuses, called with a proposition. "I've got a dog that traps mountain lions," he said. "He's a Jack Russell terrier, but he goes against cats that are four times his size. You've got to see it to believe it."

He didn't have any footage of the dog in action, but it sounded like a good idea to me. I ran it by my partners, who both agreed, so I hired a crew and took off for Lida, Nevada, in Esmeralda County, near the California border. The dog was named Mr. Chat, after the Chit-n Chat Café in Lida, and I ended up with a twenty-two-minute short subject that followed Mr. Chat as he trapped six or seven mountain lions. In the climax, ol' Mr. Chat actually fought a lion, and boy, let me tell you, the fur did fly. That lion looked huge next to Mr. Chat, but like they say in Texas: it's not the size of the dog in the fight, it's the size of the fight in the dog.

I thought the short turned out well enough that Hy Martin at Universal, who bought *Ole Rex*, might be interested. I called him, and he invited me to bring it to New York. When I arrived, I checked into the Dixie Hotel, around the corner from several studios that had offices there, including Universal and Paramount. I was so excited I woke at 7:00 the next morning, but my appointment wasn't until 1:30 that afternoon. I was afraid the anticipation would kill me before the appointed time rolled around.

Then a thought hit me. I had passed Paramount's offices on my way to the hotel, so why not call them to see if I could create a little competition? I looked up the number in the phone book and placed the call. I was taken aback when I heard a male voice on the other end of the line.

"Paramount Studios. This is Russ Holman."

As luck would have it, Holman was *the guy* in charge of acquiring short subjects. Paramount didn't ordinarily open for another hour, but he was there early to catch up on work and answered the call. When I explained what I had, he perked up.

"You got a thirty-five print?" he asked.

"Right here in my hands."

"How soon can you get here?"

I hadn't showered or shaved, but that morning I set a personal record. Within thirty minutes, I was at Paramount. Holman was in his sixties, well fed, and we hit it off real good. He led me to the projection room, gave the print to the projectionist, then we settled in to watch. I kept sneaking sideways looks at him to see if I could gauge his reaction. After about five minutes, he stopped the film.

"Oh man," I thought. "Here we go with the old 'thanks, but no thanks.'" Instead, he said, "Do you care if I bring a couple more guys up here to look at this?"

"Hell no," I thought, but I said, "Bring anyone you want."

I listened as he picked up the phone and called somebody. He gave the person the names of a couple of other guys to bring, then said, "I think we can really do something with this."

When the others arrived, we watched the short. After it ended, Holman said, "We'll buy it."

Just like that. The only problem was, I had come to New York to show it to someone else. "I have an appointment with Hy Martin at Universal. I can't sell it without running it by him first."

"I'll call Hy and tell him we want to buy it. We're really in the short subject business and Universal isn't. In fact, they lease a lot of our shorts from us. Hy will understand."

Holman ended up not only buying the short outright, but Paramount set us up on their lot in Los Angeles, with a deal to produce two shorts a year for the next four years—all with Hy Martin's blessing. As part of the deal, I agreed to accept less compensation than I originally wanted in exchange for the right to use subliminal advertising, where you use a company's product in the film but don't mention it. Nowadays most folks refer to that as "product placement." I got the idea from the medical films in which companies paid to make sure their equipment was in plain view. I figured the same principle would apply here and would more than make up for the discount I gave Paramount. Paramount's only condition was that we didn't endorse the products; we just showed them.

I started calling advertising agencies with a simple proposition: "For X amount (usually about four or five thousand dollars), we'll make sure your clients' products are seen on film by about 55 million people in over eleven countries. How does that sound?"

You sometimes hear of movies being either character-driven or plot-driven; well, our first short was product-driven. Honda had just released its Honda 125 trail bike and figured this was cheap advertising, so it jumped onboard. I came up with a story we called *The Skyline Trail*, about two guys who ride their motorcycles—Honda 125 trail bikes seemed like a good idea—from the Canadian border all the way south to the Mexican border. Along the way, they stop and eat at Kentucky Fried Chicken—*ka-ching*, another paying customer—and we also managed to capture some Chevrolets on film.

The Skyline Trail was a rousing success. Pretty soon, other companies were contacting us to use their products, but we still had our old standbys. We did one film on the Kentucky Derby, hosted and narrated by Kentucky Fried Chicken's Colonel Sanders. We did another on the Jumping Frog Jubilee in California. In that one, someone had to fly a frog from New

York to San Francisco, where a courier on a motorcycle—care
to guess the company?—picked up the frog and took him to
the fairgrounds for the jubilee. I recall that we ate chicken in
that one, too. It didn't seem right to eat frog legs.
During our four years at Paramount, the studio also used
us to shoot second-unit footage in addition to the shorts. Between that, product placement, medical films, and no overhead thanks to our studio deal, we made a nice living. Life
was good.

In 1964, Bob, Paul, and I came up with something we called
Hollywood Jamboree, essentially a country music variety show for
television. We set up a bandstand on one of the Paramount
soundstages, then filmed various artists on 16-millimeter film.
I usually shot on 35, but I planned to convert these shows to
tape for TV, and 16 was best for that.
For one of our regulars, I found a rising star named Glen
Campbell. Glen burst into prominence a few years later, in
1967, with "Gentle on My Mind" and "By the Time I Get to
Phoenix," but in 1964 he was still relatively unknown. Another of our regulars, Jeannie Seeley, also went on to stardom a couple of years later as 1966's "Most Promising New
Star," and in 1967 she won a Grammy for her number-one
song "Don't Touch Me." We ended up shooting seven *Hollywood Jamborees* that were used as network specials, and they
went over big. I have no doubt that they had something to do
with Glen's and Jeannie's huge popularity over the next few
years.
While we were working on *Hollywood Jamboree,* Elvis Presley
was filming *Paradise, Hawaiian Style* on a soundstage next door.
My buddies Red West and Charlie Hodge often hung out in
my office while Elvis was working, and sometimes Elvis hung
out with us, too. I kept a guitar there, and he would play and
we'd sing, or sometimes we'd just chew the fat. Elvis was interested in Jimmy Dean, and he asked a lot of questions about

him. It strikes me as funny that our pop culture icons have their own icons and can be as in awe of their idols as we are of them.

One day when I was in Elvis's temporary office at the studio, the publicity department sent over a framed painting of him by artist June Kelly, along with a print of the painting. "Now, what the hell am I going to do with two pictures of myself?" he asked.

"You could give one to me," I said. "You could even sign it to me."

"Give me a pen."

I did, and he signed it "To Bob, best wishes, good luck. Elvis Presley." Not real imaginative, but good enough.

I took the print to the art department to have it framed, and later that day an officious-sounding woman from the publicity department called. "Mr. Presley can't give that picture to you," she said. "That's for him."

"Well, he already gave it to me."

"If he doesn't want it, we'll give it to Mr. Wallis." Hal Wallis was Elvis's producer.

I played my trump card. "Unless Mr. Wallis's name is Bob, it's too late. Elvis already signed it to me." Then I hung up on one very ticked-off publicity department lady.

I still have that framed picture hanging on the wall over my computer today.

Another famous singer who often visited my office at Paramount was Roger Miller. One day he dropped by to see if I could cash a check for him. I took a quick look at it—$364—and thought I might be able to. I usually kept three or four hundred dollars in my money clip. I didn't have quite enough that day, but with my secretary's help, we could just cover it.

As I was counting out the money, Roger said, "I believe you're shortchanging me."

"What are you talking about? That's $364."

"You better look at the check again," he said.

I did, and I saw my mistake. It wasn't for $364; it was for $364,000—his first royalty check from "King of the Road." I had sat in with Roger when he recorded that song at the studio. Afterward, he took a cut of it back to my office, and we listened to it while we shot the breeze. Roger kept playing it over and over and over. "Why are you doing that?" I asked.

"It gives me a feel for how long folks are willing to listen to it. If I get tired of it after a few plays, I figure they will, too." Made sense to me. We stayed up late into the night, and Roger kept playing it. After what must have been the hundredth time in a row, he looked at me and said, "Hell, I still like it."

A $364,000 royalty check said the rest of the country did, too.

One of the short subjects I made was called *Dean Smith: Hollywood Stuntman*, which was narrated by Dale Robertson of *Tales of Wells Fargo* fame. Born in Breckenridge, Texas, Dean won a gold medal in the 4 × 100 meter relay at the 1952 Olympics in Helsinki, won seven Southwest Conference championships at the University of Texas, and played running back on the Longhorn football team. Later, he was drafted by the Los Angeles Rams, then was traded to the Pittsburgh Steelers, but he decided to go into the movie business instead. He found a career as an actor and stuntman that continued into the twenty-first century.

I first met Dean when I was working on a 1959 picture called *The Gunfight at Dodge City*, in which Joel McCrea played Bat Masterson. I played a small part, and Dean was an extra. When he found out I was from Texas, he introduced himself and we became friends. Now that I had my deal at Paramount, I decided Dean would be the perfect subject for a short. In 1966 I loaded my station wagon with camera and sound equipment, then drove to Austin to shoot background footage. I met up with my cameraman, Leslie Kovacs, who had flown there with his assistant.

Leslie, who later went by his given Hungarian first name Laszlo, was just starting in the business. He and I had met through a director friend of mine, and I used him on some of my medical films as well as on *Hollywood Jamboree*, where he earned his qualifications to become a member of the cinematographers' guild. He became one of the best and most successful cinematographers around. You've seen his name on films ranging from comedies like *Miss Congeniality*, *My Best Friend's Wedding*, and *Ghost Busters* to classics like *Five Easy Pieces* and *Easy Rider*. In 2002 he received a Lifetime Achievement Award from the American Society of Cinematographers.

I also used Leslie's Hungarian friend Vilmos Zsigmond, who I knew as Bill, on some of my medical films and short subjects, where he also earned his qualifications for the union. Bill and Leslie had been forced to flee Hungary for their lives, just ahead of the Russian invasion in 1956, and both men found sanctuary in the United States. Bill later received three Oscar nominations as a cinematographer and an Oscar win in 1978 for *Close Encounters of the Third Kind* (released in 1977).

From running for their lives to shooting medical films and country music specials to winning Oscars and Lifetime Achievement Awards. From humble beginnings great things come.

Leslie and his assistant rode back with me from Austin because Leslie wanted to see some of the country. I acted as tour guide, at least as we made our way across Texas. Leslie's assistant mentioned that he had heard me talking about President Lyndon Johnson as if I knew him, so he suggested we swing by the LBJ Ranch outside Stonewall, in the Texas Hill Country. I don't think he believed I actually knew LBJ, and he wanted to put me to the test. If, by chance, the president was at his "Texas White House," I could put my money where my mouth was.

I did know LBJ. I had first met him in 1957 or 1958 during the filming of *The Alamo* in Bracketville, west of San Antonio. I wasn't involved in that picture but had gone there to visit Chill Wills and some other buddies who were working on it. LBJ was still a senator, with aspirations of running for the presidency, and he came to the set one day to watch the filming. Chill and I were hanging out in Chill's room when LBJ and Bill Daniels, the brother of Texas governor Price Daniels, showed up at the door.

"I hope you boys ain't drankt all the whiskey," he boomed. No, that's not a typo; "ain't drankt" is the Texas past perfect of "drink." You might know it better as "have not drunk." We spent much of the rest of the day in Chill's room and on the set.

Later, during the Los Angeles Democratic Convention in 1960, the one that pitted LBJ against John Kennedy for the presidential nomination, I joined Chill and a few other Texans-in-Hollywood in LBJ's suite at the Ambassador Hotel. We were with the senator when Bobby Kennedy came in and told LBJ, "Jack wants to see you." When LBJ returned from meeting with John Kennedy, he told us, "Boys, I'm going to be the vice president." We were disappointed because we wanted him to be president, but, of course, he did become president a few years later.

Anyway, Leslie, his assistant, and I headed out of Austin on Highway 190 to Stonewall. I pulled up to the guardhouse at LBJ's ranch, which was manned by a Secret Service agent, appropriately dressed in the trademark dark suit, white shirt, and tie. Across the Pedernales River was the structure the media had dubbed the Texas White House. The agent approached the car, eyes narrowing suspiciously. I guess not many folks simply pulled up to the drive like that.

"Can I help you gentlemen?" he asked.

"Is the president here?" It seemed like a perfectly natural question to me, but apparently not to the Secret Service.

"Let me see your driver's license."

I gave it to him. He looked at the picture, compared it to me, then scoped out Leslie and his assistant. I knew what he was thinking: who are those bozos?

"Mr. Johnson's a friend of mine," I said. "We were just passing through and wanted to stop by and say hi if he's here."

He took my license and went into the guardhouse, where he picked up a phone. I looked at my compadres, both of whom were somewhere between disbelief and amazement. I guess ol' Leslie was really shocked. I don't suspect folks often pulled up to the leader of Hungary's house and asked to see him.

After a minute, the agent came back out. "He said to bring you to the house."

The agent searched us, then he drove us to the main house. The president stood on the huge front porch, waiting. He was dressed in khakis, boots, and a cowboy hat, as any good Texan president should be.

"Hey Bob, how you doing?" His voiced boomed out, like it always did. "When's the last time you saw ol' Chill?"

"Oh, we see each other all the time," I said.

I introduced the others to him, and he said, "You boys have a seat, and let's have some iced tea. I don't want to give you anything stronger. I wouldn't want you to get picked up by the Highway Patrol and [have to] tell them the president gave you whiskey."

We sat on the porch and drank tea, just chitchatting. He was particularly interested in hearing Leslie tell about filming the Russian invasion of Hungary that had sent him and Bill Zsigmond running for their lives.

After a while I said, "I understand you've got your own runway out there for Air Force One."

"Let me take you boys on a tour, and I'll show you. I've got some cattle I want to show you, too."

We loaded up in a white Lincoln Town Car. I sat in front with the president, while Leslie and his assistant got in the back. We followed a series of dirt maintenance roads through the ranch that I'm sure had some pattern, but it was hard to tell. He showed us the runway and was especially proud of some Santa Gertrudis cattle he had gotten from the King Ranch in south Texas.

After we'd been driving around for a while, the president pulled the car to a stop and got out. "I don't know about you boys," he said, "but I got to take a leak."

Before the rest of us could react, he had started. Well, when in Rome . . .

When we left, the president saw us off. "Good luck," he said. "Tell ol' Chill I said hi."

After we got on the road, no one said anything at first. Leslie rode beside me, his assistant in the back. Then I heard this noise from behind me. I looked in the rearview mirror, and that fella was laughing so hard I thought he was going to cry. "What's so funny?" I asked.

It was all he could do to talk. "None of my friends are going to believe me when I tell them that we had some iced tea and took a leak with the president of the United States."

Well, that set all three of us off. We must have laughed for the next fifteen miles. He was right as hell. No one was going to believe us.

And we surely didn't have any pictures to prove it.

CHAPTER SIXTEEN

Jumping, Singing, Suing, and Gambling

Well, you know, he's just a lawyer. He doesn't make the
jumps, and he doesn't take the falls. He doesn't know what
it's worth.

—EVEL KNIEVEL

One day in April 1968, I was in my office on Ventura
Boulevard, next to CBS, when a young guy pulled up in
an old Rolls Royce. The car got my attention, but I didn't have
any appointments scheduled. I watched the driver as he got
out with crutches, which seemed odd for a man that young.
He walked as if he had suffered an injury, but I didn't see any
casts, just the crutches. I didn't know if he was headed my way,
but I waited to see. A few minutes later I heard him talking to
my secretary, then she led him in.

"You Bob Hinkle?" he asked.

"I am."

"My name is Bobby Knievel. Jim Jernigan over in Las
Vegas said I should talk to you."

Jernigan specialized in booking lounge acts in Vegas, and
I had met him while visiting Benny Binion.

"I want you to help me make my name as big as Elvis," the
young man continued.

"You sing and play guitar?"

"No."

I eyed his cane. "Doesn't look like you dance either."

"No, sir. I jump motorcycles."

That rang a bell. "You mean you ride motorcycles and jump over things?"

"Yes, sir."

"Over what?"

"Cars, trucks, rattlesnake pits. You name it, I'll jump over it. People will pay good money to see that."

"What happened to you?" I asked.

"If you've got a projector, I've got a piece of film to show you."

I set it up, and he showed me the most spectacular piece of footage I'd ever seen. Some of you will remember Bobby's jump over the fountains at Caesar's Palace in Las Vegas in late 1967. He cleared the fountains, but something went wrong on the landing. He wobbled on the motorcycle for a second, then pitched headfirst over the handlebars. His body bounced like a crash test dummy, finally rolling to a stop. If you hadn't seen the actual jump but just the fall, you'd never believe that was a human being flopping around in the parking lot. It damn near broke the egg in him, and he ended up in a coma for about a month.

But it also made him famous, and now he was asking me to help him capitalize on that. He was going by the easy-to-promote nickname "Evel," and we hit on the idea of making a documentary-style movie about him. Using the same approach I employed in my short subjects, our plan was to shoot a lot of footage of his jumps, then edit that together with narration I would write. We didn't have a written contract, only a handshake, but a shake was as good as my name on paper, so I figured the same ought to be true for him. We would be 50–50 partners in the movie—provided we could get it off the ground, so to speak. That meant we had to start promoting Evel right away, to take advantage of his spectacular crash at

Caesar's Palace that was still fresh on America's collective mind.

I started by calling Merv Griffin. Merv wasn't too sure about putting a motorcycle jumper on his show, but I twisted his arm until he agreed. "I'll give him three minutes," he said, probably wondering how he was going to fill the last two after showing the footage. It turned out that he didn't have to worry. Merv was so taken with Evel that the time stretched into ten-and-a-half minutes.

Then we started setting up jumps at racetracks around the country. We began in Albuquerque, and Evel showed me that he already knew plenty about promotion. He called the owner of the track and, speaking in a disguised voice, said, "I'm Evel Knievel's manager, and we'd like to go for the world record of jumping over thirteen cars. Are you interested in letting us do it at your track?"

"You bet," the owner said.

"Evel charges fifty cents a head. Tack that on to your regular ticket price, and we've got a deal."

After he hung up, Evel said, "You know, he went for that too fast. I think he'd have gone a dollar if I'd asked for it."

"It's too late now. You've already made your deal."

"Oh yeah? Watch this." He waited about fifteen minutes and called back to the Albuquerque track. This time he introduced himself as Evel, then said, "Listen, my attorney said he made a deal with you for fifty cents a head. Is that right?"

"Yes sir. Just a little while ago."

"Well, you know, he's just a lawyer. He doesn't make the jumps, and he doesn't take the falls. He doesn't know what it's worth. I've got to have a dollar a head if I'm going to go for the world record. People will pay for the chance to see something like what happened at Caesar's Palace."

And just like that, he made a new bargain. Then he contacted the leading Ford dealership in Albuquerque and made another deal. "I've been jumping Chevrolets, but I want to switch to Fords, since that's what I drive," Evel said. "If you'll put a little note in the corner of your newspaper ads about the jump, then we'll jump your Fords, and you can use that to promote your dealership."

The guy went for it, and we set a track record in Albuquerque of over 5,500 spectators, all of whom were more than happy to pay that dollar to see Evel jump. For the price, they would either get to see a spectacular stunt or a spectacular fall. From then on, we required that all the owners tack on a dollar for every jump. Some of them might have been skeptical at first, but word got around about the motorcycle jumping, which usually ended up being a bigger attraction than the actual races. We drew a crowd of 21,000 in Seattle, where Evel set a record by jumping fourteen cars.

We even figured out how to get free room and board at Holiday Inns in the jump cities by promoting the fact that Evel was staying there. Sometimes we got his name on billboards at the hotels, welcoming him, and I'd pretend to roll cameras as the hotel managers greeted their star guest when he checked in. I say "pretend" because we never actually filmed any of those "greets." I didn't want to waste such a valuable commodity as film on something we had no intention of using.

Most folks have phobias of one kind or another. We're all afraid of something, from spiders and snakes to heights or crowds. I'm no psychiatrist, and I don't know what you'd call it, but I believe that Evel Knievel had a bona fide phobia that he was going to die and still have money in his bank account. He seemed determined to spend every dollar he took in, as if he wanted his funeral expenses to drain his last penny. And he damn near did it.

When the Evel Knievel action figure almost single-handedly saved the Mattel Toy Company, 1970 became a very good year for Evel financially. It pumped up his bank account, and he needed help getting rid of some of that money.

"Come on, Bob," he said. "Let's go to Vegas."

What better place to open up a financial vein and bleed dollars? When we hit town, we went to the Sands, where Evel promptly cashed a twenty-five thousand dollar check and almost as promptly lost about fifteen thousand of it at the dice tables. We piled back into our limo—another good way to get rid of money is to hire a limo just to tote you from casino to casino—and headed to Caesar's Palace. As we drove the strip, we looked at the lines of tourists and locals—a lot of them obviously working people—walking from one casino to the next while we were chauffeured in luxury. Evel popped the band off a pack of one hundred dollar bills—five thousand dollars in all—and tossed the bills out the window. They scattered like confetti as people scrambled into our wake, grasping for those C notes.

"What the hell did you do that for?" I asked.

"They need it worse than I do."

I needed it worse than he did, too, but he hadn't bothered to toss a bundle in my lap.

I first met the actor George Hamilton during the filming of *All the Fine Young Cannibals*. More recently, he'd been involved in a short-lived series called *The Survivors*, and in 1970 he was working on another, called *Paris 7000*, for Universal. He called me one day and said, "Bob, I'd sure like to have Evel double for me in the new series on some stunts. You think he'd be interested?"

I knew that was bull. George was a self-promoter, and word had it he wanted to do a movie about Evel. He figured if he got Evel a spot on his show, Evel would owe him a favor. But we agreed because it was a gig for Evel, and we'd take all we could get. It also might help to have George or even Universal backing Evel. We decided to shoot something that not only George could use but that we could use, too.

Bob and George Hamilton, on the set of the movie *Evel Knievel* (1970). Courtesy of Bob Hinkle.

In the footage, shot in Sacramento, Evel makes a jump, then the scene cuts to George riding out from behind a building, and it looks like he made the jump. The film looked good, but Universal canceled the television show after about ten episodes and moved George off the lot. That left us with this segment of George pretending to jump a motorcycle and nothing for either George or us to promote. Or so we thought.

Without telling me, George took the footage to a fellow named Joe Solomon, who had executive produced a bunch of biker movies. None of them were serious pictures, but Solomon had a reputation for getting things made that involved motorcycles, and George thought he was a natural for the Evel Knievel story. Solomon's first question, when he saw my name on the film, was, "Who's Robert Hinkle?"

"He's the guy who works with Evel. He put this whole thing together."

"Yeah, but we're not going to use this footage. We'll come up with our own script. F—— Hinkle. Let him sue us if he doesn't like it."

It apparently suited George just fine to cut me out, which tells you all you need to know about him. But let me tell you more. George's mother had married a truck driver named Spalding, who had nothing to do with Spalding Sporting Goods, but George wasn't above letting people think he came from Spalding money. When I first met him on *Cannibals*, he didn't even have a car. Sometimes I gave him a ride home at the end of the day, even though it was out of my way. His mother often house-sat for wealthy families, and George led people to believe he lived in the fancy houses I took him to. I'm not saying George was a phony; I'm just telling you what I know. You can draw your own conclusions.

When I heard that Joe Solomon was going forward with a movie about Evel, starring George Hamilton, and was cutting me out, I was PO'd. I went to my attorney, Averill Paserow, to see if I had any legal grounds to stay attached.

"There's not much you can do to stop them from making the movie," he said. "But if you wait until they release it, then you've got leverage. If it's a hit, they'll have to settle rather than let you get an injunction or go to trial for a portion of the profits. I'll draft the lawsuit, but let's wait to file it."

Sure enough, when the movie came out it was a big hit, and Averill filed the lawsuit. Very early the next morning I got a phone call from New York. Robert Fryer, a Broadway producer who won a Tony Award for his musical production of *Wonderful Town* and who also produced films, was on the other end. "What are you going to do with that $6 million?" he asked.

"What $6 million?"

"There's an AP news story breaking that you're suing George Hamilton and Joe Solomon and that you're going to get an injunction on the Knievel movie, and you're asking for $6 million."

Even though we named Evel as a defendant, it was a friendly suit against him. Our real targets were Hamilton and Solomon. Averill was right; they made a nice settlement—not for $6 million, of course, but I never expected that—and I was happy to get the cash. I was also supposed to get a percentage of the profits, but to this day I haven't received a penny from the movie. The experience left a sour taste in my mouth for the ways of Hollywood and a less than stellar opinion of George Hamilton.

I first met Benny Binion through Chill Wills, who had been a friend of Benny's since his Dallas days, where he made his name as a gambler before being forced to flee the state one step ahead of the law. He ended up in Las Vegas and ultimately opened the Horseshoe Casino. In 1970 the Horseshoe sponsored the first World Championship of Poker, with Chill as the host. Benny asked me to take still pictures of the games for a brochure he wanted to put together, which I was happy to do.

Chill and I arrived early to set things up, and Benny introduced me to Titanic Thompson, whom he had flown in from Grapevine, Texas, for the tournament. "Ti," whose real name was Alvin C. Thomas, was pushing eighty by then, but he had been a gambler and golf hustler extraordinaire from practically the day he was born. He was supposedly involved in the murder of Arnold Rothstein, the man behind fixing the 1919 World Series that forever tainted the Chicago "Black" Sox and the reputation of Shoeless Joe Jackson. There was never any real evidence to connect Ti to Rothstein's murder, but he was more than happy to milk that reputation as part of his mystery.

First Poker Tournament, Binion's Horseshoe Club, Las Vegas (1970). Hold 'Em winner Johnny Moss, third from left, with Chill Wills, Benny Binion, and Ti Thompson to his right. Courtesy of Bob Hinkle.

Ti Thompson stories were legend in those days. He would bet on just about anything. He would even bet on the bets. "Propositions," he called them. He also made sure the odds were always in his favor. If they weren't, he fixed them so they were. One story had him betting on the distance to Dallas from Tyler, in east Texas. A highway sign he and his traveling companion passed said "Dallas 88." "I think that sign's wrong," Ti said. "I'll bet you it's less than seventy-five miles to the court-house in Dallas." A wager was made, the trip was clocked, and the distance came in at something like seventy-three miles. Ti's companion paid up, unaware that the night before, Ti had left his Tyler hotel room in the middle of the night, driven to the highway, uprooted the mileage sign, and trans-planted it fifteen miles closer to Dallas.

On another wager, this one made in the middle of winter, Ti bet a group of gambling golfers in Chicago that he could drive a golf ball off a regulation tee at least five hundred yards. "I'll be going for distance, not style," he said, "so is it all right if it doesn't stay on the fairway?" No one had any quarrel with that. "And I get to choose the course and the hole?" Again, no quarrel, so the bet was made. Ti loaded up the pigeons (Ti always considered himself the hawk in the midst of pigeons), and they went to a course on the edge of frozen Lake Michigan. Ti teed up on a hole adjacent to the lake, then turned around and drove his ball onto the ice, where it hit, skipped, and rolled for about a mile.

I spent three fascinating days with Ti and even played golf with him. That old man could still play golf like an SOB. He had ground down a heel on his shoe, and he could putt with that heel. He'd bet you that he could putt the ball closer to a hole with his heel than you could with your putter, a bet he nearly always won.

As Benny and I sat at a table in the Horseshoe one evening, listening to Titanic Thompson telling his stories, I said, "If I had the money, I'd buy the rights to your life."

"I'll take twenty-five thousand dollars for them."

Benny immediately left the table, returned a few minutes later with twenty-five thousand in hundred dollar bills, and gave it to me. "I want you to do a picture up there on my ranch, and here's the down-payment on it."

I paid that money to Ti, Benny had a lawyer friend draft the contract, and I bought outright the "entire worldwide, absolute, unqualified, sole and exclusive rights," including the rights to "all legendary schemes and exploits," to the life of Alvin C. Thomas. If it's the last thing I do, I still intend to bring that story to the big screen.

Back in 1957, Albert Gannaway had directed a picture in Kanab, Utah, called *The Badge of Marshall Brennan*, starring B western actors like Jim Davis and Lee Van Cleef, and he had rounded up a bunch of country singers to play the other parts. Van Cleef was later known for his work with Clint Eastwood in Sergio Leone's spaghetti westerns, like *For a Few Dollars More* and *The Good, the Bad, and the Ugly*. Davis later played Jock Ewing, Sr., in the mega-hit TV series *Dallas*.

Al managed to commit an unpardonable sin in the middle of production: he ran out of film. This was before I knew Al, but I knew Bill Ward, his stunt coordinator, who called me to fly five thousand feet of 35-millimeter film to Utah. With my buddy Whitey Hughes in tow, I rented a Piper Tri-Pacer airplane at Van Nuys Airport, and we delivered the film. While we were there, Al hired me to double for Jim Davis in a fight scene, while Bill Coontz doubled for Van Cleef. I jumped off a rock onto Bill and we had a fight, and I pocketed $250 for an hour's work. Then it was time to head back to Los Angeles.

One of the country singers Al used was Webb Pierce, a Grand Ole Opry regular who was famous for such hits as "In the Jailhouse Now" and "Why, Baby, Why?" "I've got to get back to the Opry," Webb said to me. "Can you drop my wife and me off in Vegas on your way back so we can catch a plane to Nashville?"

"That won't be a problem," I lied. It was a lie because although Tri-Pacers have seats for four, they won't carry much weight. Between Whitey and me, we almost overloaded it ourselves, but we piled Webb and his wife, Audrey, into the back and took off. I say "took off," but that's mighty generous. The runway ended at a steep drop-off, and when we reached it we dropped all right.

And dropped and dropped.

More than one hillbilly singer like Webb had died in a plane crash, and I knew that had to be pressing on his mind. He leaned forward, his eyes as big as bowling balls. "What happens if the engine stops?"

"Then we'll be doing a lot of loud singing and slow walking." I could see that wasn't very reassuring to him.

I was finally able to pull up enough to get over the mountains, and we held our breaths all the way back to Las Vegas, where I landed without having to use flaps. We touched down, then rolled about a hundred yards before we reached a dead stop. I was never so happy to be on solid ground again. We had, I believe, escaped death. But I got another little adventure to add to my life's story, and I got to do a little work and come back $250 richer.

And I also got to meet a man who would become one of my dearest friends. Another of the country singers Al used on the picture was Marty Robbins, who was relatively unknown at the time. Marty and I became friendly on the Utah set, and, after that, any time he came to Los Angeles, we'd get together. From there, our friendship took off.

One day in 1968, Marty's manager, Marty Landow, called me to pick the two of them up at the Los Angeles airport. Landow lived in L.A., while Marty lived in Nashville. The two had met in Phoenix for a concert, then flew to Los Angeles together.

Landow lived on Coldwater Canyon Road, about a mile-and-a-half from the Howard Johnson's where Marty was staying. As we approached Landow's house, I jokingly said, "All you've got is that hanging bag, so I'll just get off the freeway here and let you walk home, then I can get back on real quick."

I thought it was obvious that I was joking, but Landow didn't seem to think so. "No, Bob, I'm not feeling too good. I really need you to take me home."

I had noticed that he seemed quiet during the drive, so I didn't say anything more. Later that night, Landow apparently had trouble sleeping, so he got up and made himself a pot of coffee, then sat in his home office, coffee cup in front of him—and promptly had a heart attack and died. When his wife found him the next morning, he was still sitting at his desk, coffee cold, with his head slumped forward. She thought he was asleep, so she went to make breakfast. When she tried to wake him later, she discovered he was dead. She ran next door in a panic to Tommy Thomas's apartment. Tommy ran the Palomino Club, a nightclub for country music, and was friends with the Landows. He didn't know where Marty Robbins was staying, but he had my phone number, so he called right away.

I immediately called Marty. "I've got some bad news," I said, "but I'm not going to tell you on the phone. I'm on my way to pick you up right now, so get dressed."

It scared the hell out of him. His wife and kids always contacted me if they needed to get a message to him, so his natural first thought was that something had happened to one of them. He was waiting out front when I got there.

"What's wrong?" he asked when he got in the car.

"Marty Landow died."

It was as though he couldn't understand what I had said. "What?"

"Marty Landow had a heart attack and died last night. He's still in his office."

We got to Landow's before the police arrived, but they ran us off so they could take care of the body. Marty and I were both in shock. We didn't know what to do because Landow had been his manager for a lot of years and knew his business affairs inside and out.

"Bob," Marty said, "you've got to help me get my contracts and appearances straightened out."

"Sure I will."

"We need to get his Rolodex and my contracts. And we need to get my bank accounts changed out. Marty was handling everything through his trust accounts."

We took care of those things, and later Marty asked me to be his manager. I didn't think I had the expertise, but Marty insisted. "I'll tell you what to say and what to do. That way I don't have to be the heavy. I'll even put you on salary, so that'll be a deduction for me, and it works for everybody."

I reluctantly agreed to do it for one year on a trial basis, and that one year turned into more than a decade. Every January he paid me in advance for the upcoming year, all with nothing more than a handshake.

"What if I die before the year's up?" I asked him once.

"Your wife can use the rest of it." That's the kind of man Marty Robbins was.

I negotiated all of Marty's film and television deals, and we worked together on various projects of our own. I had a good rapport with the folks at Universal, which owned MCA, so when Marty's contract expired at Columbia I set him up at Universal. Part of the arrangement was a requirement that if Marty and I made any movies together, Universal would release them.

On New Year's Day 1971, Marty called me with an idea for a movie about country music. I met him in Nashville, where he explained the storyline about a writer, ultimately played in the movie by a well-known Los Angeles disc jockey named Sammy Jackson, who was doing a story on country music. He

On the set of *Country Music* (1972). *Left to right:* Bob, Marty Robbins, and Sammy Jackson. Courtesy of Bob Hinkle.

would follow a country singer, played by Marty, around as he toured. It's similar in concept to Cameron Crowe's *Almost Famous* (2000), about a young kid hired by *Rolling Stone Magazine* to tour with a rock band and write a story about it. We called ours *Country Music.* I produced and directed, while Marty starred and Universal released it. We used other country stars as well, like Barbara Mandrell and Shelly West, and had a lot of fun.

In 1973 Marty and I produced another picture that was going to be one of the last of the Gene Autry/Roy Rogers–style "singing westerns." Marty had released an album called *Drifter* in 1966, and we were going to use that title, as well as the songs from the album, as our soundtrack. However, Clint Eastwood was making *High Plains Drifter* at the same time we were shooting. Universal convinced us to change the title, and we came up with *Guns of a Stranger* instead. I directed and Marty starred as Sheriff Matthew Roberts. I got to use a lot of my old buddies, like Chill and Bill Coontz, and I even used my daughter, Melody, who played the wife of Marty's son, Robbie.

Look closely at video of Marty before and after late 1974, and you'll notice a difference in his appearance. His face doesn't seem as round, and his nostrils don't flare as much. Marty always hated those nostrils. He said his nose looked like an empty two-car garage with the doors open. But after 1974, the garage appeared to have been narrowed. You might think the change was simply a result of the mustache he took to wearing—most people do—but I'll let you in on a little secret: it's not.

Marty was a big fan of stock car racing and did some racing of his own. On October 6, 1974, he was in a wreck in Charlotte, North Carolina, that left him with pretty bad lacerations on his forehead and nose. He came to Los Angeles, and I introduced him to a plastic surgeon. You know how any time you do a home improvement project it seems to grow? The new kitchen floor looks so good, you think you need new cabinets. And with those new cabinets, now you need new appliances. And now the dining room looks outdated, so you've got to improve that. And so on and so on. Well, that's kinda how this went.

"Think you can narrow Marty's nose when you fix those scars?" I asked the doctor.

"That won't be a problem."

"Can you do something about those bags under his eyes?"

"We can take care of that, too."

Then Marty got onboard, talking about the roundness of his face and the wrinkles on his forehead, and next thing you knew, he'd had a complete facelift. That created a new problem: Marty had come to Los Angeles with one face, and he'd be leaving with another. I had a suggestion. "It's going to take about a month for all that swelling and bruising from the surgery to heal," I said. "Why don't you grow a mustache? People are going to know something's different, but maybe they'll think it's just the new growth."

Marty liked that idea just fine. He called his wife, Marizona, and told her he'd be in Los Angeles for a while, but he didn't tell her about the facelift. He stayed in the Howard Johnson's for a month while he healed and grew his mustache. I brought him food and pain pills as needed. By the time he was back in circulation, he had a fully grown mustache.

"Marty," people said, "that mustache makes you look a lot younger. It really looks good on you."

What a difference a mustache makes.

One of my most prized possessions is a letter Marty wrote to me on December 15, 1979. It was completely unsolicited, came out of the blue, but I treasure it to this day. He wrote:

Dear Bob,

First, I would like to thank you for your friendship for the past 23 years. It has been very reassuring to know someone who has been so loyal and trustworthy to my company and to my family.

I appreciate the sacrifices you made in your own personal life to be available, sometimes at a moment's notice, for my personal appearances or to be with me at my stock-car racing.

Most of all, many thanks for the great job you did as my Personal Manager for eleven years, which I feel was a definite asset to enhancing my career.

I know our friendship and association will continue for many years to come.

Your friend always,

Marty Robbins

CHAPTER SEVENTEEN

Some Memories
Never Die

I would like to be remembered as a good entertainer, a good
person. I think, maybe better as a good person.

—MARTY ROBBINS

If you were to ask me what my job was between 1952 and
1973, I'd tell you I was in the picture business, even if not
always directly so. It kept me hopping, but I always made time
for my family. Both Brad and Mike were baseball players, and
I coached their teams as they moved through Little League
and Babe Ruth League. Because I was my own boss during
their teenage years, I was able to schedule my work around
their games and practices, careful never to miss one if I could
help it.

I guess my involvement in the picture business had some
influence on the kids because even though Mike, my oldest,
joined the U.S. Air Force after graduating from high school in
1970, followed by two years of junior college, and went on to
become a laboratory technician, both Melody and Brad ended
up in the business. As I mentioned, Melody was in *Guns of a
Stranger*, and in 1976 she played one of the Manson Family
girls in *Helter Skelter*, based on prosecutor Vincent Bugliosi's
best-selling book. She also got involved in a workshop pro-
gram at CBS and appeared in such series as *Laverne and Shirley*

234

Bob with his sons, Brad and Mike, in their Little League uniforms (1962). Courtesy of Bob Hinkle.

Bob's family in Brownfield, Texas (1960). Courtesy of Bob Hinkle.

and *The Brady Bunch.* She ultimately left acting after getting married.

Brad, my younger son, turned down a baseball scholarship to USC in 1972 for a job in the lighting and electrical department at Universal Studios. It was a tough choice because he loved baseball, but he felt that if he learned a trade, a career in the movie business offered more security than baseball did. As a pitcher, he would always be just one arm injury away from being out of the sport. The decision paid off, and over the years he worked on a number of Hollywood's biggest hits, including *Jaws, Close Encounters of the Third Kind,* and *Earthquake.*

If you were to ask me what my job was between 1973 and when I finally retired (or semi-retired, anyway) in 1994, the answer wouldn't be so simple. Marty's and my deal with Universal expired in 1975, and I had started looking at other pursuits. Hollywood had pretty well burned me out. I don't know how much of that had to do with the movie about Evel Knievel and the subsequent lawsuit, but over the next two decades my interests bounced around, much like the pinball machine I referenced earlier when describing the impossibility of plotting your course in the picture business. A grown man ought to know what he wants to do with his life, but I didn't—at least not for long—as I moved from job to job. What I realize in hindsight is that I was simply working my way back home to Texas, though in a roundabout way.

I was starting to dabble in a number of things, some of them still related to the movie business—if only peripherally—but some of them not even close. We made the movie Benny Binion had put the down-payment on, about a cattle roundup and branding, which we filmed at his ranch in Jordan, Montana. Chill drove the chuck wagon and narrated, while I handled the actual production. We ended up with a thirty-minute picture called *Binion Big Country.* I don't know what Benny did with it, but I got paid so I didn't care.

In 1973, five-time world all-around rodeo champion Larry Mahan made his comeback and battled it out with Phil Lyne to win his sixth championship. Documentary director Kieth Merrill followed their competition for a documentary called *The Great American Cowboy.* I filmed several of the rodeos, including those at Cheyenne, the Cow Palace, and Pecos, Texas, for the documentary, which won an Academy Award for Kieth in 1974. I like to think I had at least a small part in that Oscar.

While flying around with Larry, I met a fellow named Bob Cook, who owned a stock-contracting business in Clements, California. He was getting ready to take a Wild West show and rodeo to Taiwan, of all places. He hired me to run the physical show while he handled the business end of things. Can you imagine a Wild West show in Asia? But he thought he could make some money at it, so I went with him. We were in Taiwan about six weeks and drew crowds by the thousands. It seems as if the whole world loves cowboys.

I had gotten my start in rodeo as a calf roper, and the last calf I ever roped was in Taiwan. I had taken leave of my senses, so I decided I'd try one more shot at my old specialty for the Chinese crowd. I rode my horse in and roped the calf smooth as can be. I still had it! But when I jumped off my horse, I landed awkwardly. I stumbled, then took a pratfall. Pretty embarrassing for a west Texas calf roper, but the crowd seemed to like it. I managed to get to my feet and grab the rope, only to fall again. The people in the stands went crazy. They had no interest in seeing a calf roped and tied in eight seconds. They thought that was too fast. Fortunately for them, unfortunately for me, I accommodated them by dragging this particular roping out.

The way it's supposed to work is your horse backs up to keep the rope taut while you throw the calf down and tie it up. My horse must not have known that because he kept coming forward while I was fighting with the calf, and the slack gave the calf more room to get away. I finally got that sucker tied, but it might've taken a minute and a half or longer. I got a standing ovation from the crowd, though. They thought it was the funniest thing they'd ever seen.

Bob Hinkle, comic relief.

Larry Mahan asked me to help him find a house in Los Angeles. My wife and daughter were working in real estate at the time, so I found myself interested in the field. Result: I got my real estate license and sold the homes of such Hollywood notables as James Brolin. When the real estate market tapered off in 1978, I decided to go to auctioneer school in Billings, Montana, then I came back to Los Angeles and sold houses at auction. That worked for a while, but my interest soon waned, and it was time for yet another career change.

In 1979 I was visiting my mother and sister in Washington and noticed there was no place to get barbecue. To an ol' boy from Texas that was a damn tragedy, and I got the notion to put in a barbecue pit. I found a building near Fort Lewis and McCord Air Force Base in Tacoma that looked like an ideal location. I knew there were a lot of service folks from the South who were probably homesick, and I figured they'd like a little barbecue as a reminder of home. I bought the building and turned it into Texas Bob's Bar B Q. I mean, we did a landslide business, with good Texas barbecue, Texas chili, homemade apple cobbler, and Texas pecan pie as our specialties.

We made the local Tacoma television after the crew of *PM Magazine* pulled in to eat one day. I had lined the walls of the restaurant with pictures from my years in the movie business, and that caught the eye of the producer, who came back a couple of weeks later and did a show. After it aired, customers lined up early the next day, down the block for about a half-mile. By one o'clock I had sold all the barbecue I had planned on for the entire day. That became a regular occurrence, and my business tripled almost overnight. The ultimate result was a raft of offers to buy me out.

In 1980 I claimed a racehorse named Seven Come Eleven at Long Acres track in Seattle. She was an older mare, and I ran her in Washington throughout 1980 and into 1981, then shipped her to Bay Meadows in San Francisco to run. I decided to follow her to California and go back to Los Angeles, so I called this ol' boy who had been dogging me to buy the restaurant and threw an arbitrary number, with some conditions attached, on the table. Damned if he didn't take it.

Back in Hollywood, Paramount hired me to shoot second-unit stuff and stock footage, which I did until the end of 1986. That helped me put my own film library together. Also in the 1980s, Snuff Garrett, whom I had known for years from his days producing at Liberty Records, hired me as a technical adviser and sales manager for Bohlin Silver Saddles & Buckles in Los Angeles. Snuff had Texas roots. He was born in Dallas and worked as a disc jockey in Wichita Falls and Lubbock before coming west. Burt Reynolds was one of his partners in the business, which made saddles, belt buckles, and western wear.

I had a lot of fun working at Bohlin because if there was anything I knew, it was western attire. It gave me a chance to indulge my creative side as I designed belt buckles for movie stars like my friends Robert Wagner and Natalie Wood. Sadly, Natalie died before I finished hers. I also designed buckles for athletes, including USC quarterback Vince Evans, who had played in four Rose Bowls. The buckle I designed for him had four roses on it. I even designed one for O. J. Simpson, though I guess he won't need it anymore.

After Snuff closed Bohlin in 1985, I worked for a friend named Cotton Rosser, handling public relations work for the Flying U Rodeo in Marysville, near Sacramento, and the National Finals Rodeo in Las Vegas. I didn't much care for that job because it had me on the road too much. At the end of the year, I told Cotton I was ready to move on, and he was okay with that.

What I really wanted to do—or thought I wanted to do— was get back into the restaurant business. I bought the Porter House Restaurant in Moses Lake, Washington, but after about two years I got antsy again. When Marty Robbins's son called at the end of 1988 and asked me to help him put some shows together, I agreed. I sold the restaurant, and we moved to

Nashville. I had barely hit the city limits when Al Gannaway at Network One offered me the job of general manager for the network that later became TNN. I worked at Network One through 1991, then segued into doing country music videos, which TNN really popularized. That was my last stop before returning to Texas.

Like I said, this period of time was a regular potpourri of activity that defies classification. It was an exciting time for me, but it was also a sad time because I lost a few more old friends.

In late 1976 or early 1977 I flew to Memphis to meet with the folks at Holiday Inn to see about using their hotels in a short subject. I happened to be on the same plane with my old buddy Red West, and we got to talking about Elvis. I hadn't seen Elvis in a while; in fact, nobody had seen much of him, and rumors abounded about his health, weight, drug use—if there was any aspect of his life that folks could spread rumors about, then that's exactly what they did.

"How's he doing?" I asked.

"Not too good," Red said. "He's getting so fat you wouldn't believe it. All he does is hang out and eat all night, then sleep all day. He's like a hermit."

About 10:00 that night, after I was already in bed at my hotel, the phone rang. It was Red. "El wants to see you," he said.

I immediately jumped up and got dressed, then grabbed a cab to Graceland. Red ushered me inside. It was after 10:30, and Red, Charlie Hodge, Lamar Fike (another of Elvis's entourage), and I shot the breeze while we waited for Elvis . . . and waited . . . and waited.

Finally, around midnight, Elvis came down the stairs. I knew from what Red had told me that he had let himself go, but I wasn't prepared for the bloated man I saw. He hugged me, then held me at arm's length, as if to see if I was as fat as he was. I wasn't, not by a long shot.

"Stay and have supper with us," he said.

Supper? Hell, it was damn near time for breakfast! But who was I to argue a fine point like that?

Elvis's cook fried up a batch of pork chops, some mashed potatoes and gravy, biscuits—a good southern supper—at 12:30 A.M. Just in case I wondered how he'd gotten so fat.

"This is the last time I'm gonna eat like this," Elvis said. "I'm gonna get myself back in shape and go on tour again."

I could see from the faces of the others at the table that they might have heard that line before. But I played along.

"Marty's got another song for you," I said. Elvis had already had one hit with Marty's "You Gave Me a Mountain."

"Have him get it over to Felton Jarvis." Elvis's producer.

I made the promise, then the conversation turned to other things. As we talked and ate, I couldn't help feeling sorry for him. He was still Elvis, but he wasn't the Elvis he had once been. I knew he longed to be that Elvis again. Roger Miller said it best, and I'm sure Elvis was probably thinking the same thing: "I'd give all the money back if I could just have one more hit."

Elvis died a few months later, in August 1977, before Marty got the chance to get that song to Jarvis. It was called "The Entertainer," and although Marty ended up recording it himself, it was never released.

In early December 1982, Marty called me for a big favor. For some time, he had been addicted to Valium. His doctor initially prescribed the pills to help him sleep, and Marty soon found himself hooked, even relying on them to get him through his concerts. He would pop a pill about forty-five minutes before going on stage, which sometimes made it look as if he were performing drunk.

"Bob, I want you to rent a place in L.A. for a month, and I'll come out after the first of the year and kick these pills."

I was never happier to do him a favor than I was that one, so I rented an apartment on Barham Boulevard, near Warner Brothers Studio. I couldn't wait for January 1 to arrive, but I had other business to attend to in the meantime. I was going to the National Finals Rodeo in Oklahoma City to shoot footage for a couple of the cowboys, including Donnie Gay. Donnie was from Mesquite, Texas, and he ultimately won the world bull riding championship eight times.

The following Saturday, the day before I left for Oklahoma City, Marty called again. His voice was strained and his breathing uneven, as if he was in pain. "Bob," he said, "my chest feels like it's going to blow up."

Those words sucked the wind out of me. Marty had suffered a couple of heart attacks, including one just a year earlier, and had already had a triple bypass, so nothing he could say would have scared me more.

"I'm lying on the kitchen floor right now because it's the only place I can get comfortable."

"Marty, you've got to call your doctor right now."

"I hate to do that. He works all week, and the weekend's the only time he gets off. But I'll call him first thing Monday morning."

Despite my protests, Marty hung tough. I flew to Oklahoma City, but my thoughts constantly strayed to him. He called his doctor the next Monday, as he had promised. The doctor immediately asked to talk to Marizona. "I don't mean to scare you," he said, "but this is serious. Get him in the car and bring him to my office. I'll have an ambulance waiting."

Marty lived in Franklin, Tennessee, about thirty miles out in the country from Nashville, and his doctor's office was about midway between Marty's house and the closest hospital, which was Saint John's. Marizona helped Marty as he literally crawled on his hands and knees to the car, and she rushed him to a waiting ambulance at the doctor's office.

When they finally got Marty on the operating table at Saint John's, the surgeons discovered multiple blocked arteries. He suffered a massive heart attack during the surgery, and, after a quadruple bypass, he was put on life support.

I spoke to his doctors several times over the next few days, and each time the report was the same: no improvement. The folks at the hospital told me only family members were allowed in the ICU, but I couldn't stand it any longer. I found a late night flight and headed to Nashville, arriving damn near in the middle of the night. I got to Saint John's around 2:30 A.M. and went straight to the ICU, where a nurse stopped me.

"Is any of the family here?" I asked.

"They left about an hour ago to get some rest."

"Well, I'm his manager. Better'n that, I'm his friend. I flew in just to see him."

She hesitated for a bit, and I knew she was thinking about it. Finally she said, "We're both going to get in trouble if we get caught, but come with me."

She led me into the ICU, which was a succession of single-bed rooms along a corridor, filled with patients hooked up to enough equipment to send an astronaut to the moon and back. An old man who looked as if he might be a hundred years old occupied the bed in the first room. I was shocked when the nurse said, "He's right here."

My knees nearly buckled as I looked at my friend. I wouldn't have recognized him if my life depended on it.

"Take his hand and talk to him," she said.

I picked up his lifeless hand, stunned by how cold it felt. "Marty," I said, "do you know who this is?"

I felt a pressure on my hand. Not much, but I knew he was squeezing "yes."

I had to be sure it wasn't just a reflex. "Is this Bobby Sykes?" I asked, naming another of his friends.

No reaction.

"Dan Winters?"

Nothing.

"Bob Hinkle?"

There was that squeeze! Hell yes, he knew who I was.

I stayed for only about ten or fifteen minutes, talking gently to him, before the nurse insisted I had to leave. I caught a plane back to Oklahoma City, where I got word the next day that Marty had died.

December 8, 1982.

Seeing Marty in the hospital, feeling him squeeze my hand, seems just as real today as it did then. More than that, it seems like it was just yesterday, even though more than a quarter of a century has passed. One of Marty's last big hits, a song written for him by Bobby Springfield, sums up my feelings as I think of him. Even though it was written as a song about lost romantic love, it applies equally to me. The title says it all: "Some Memories Just Won't Die."

CHAPTER EIGHTEEN

Going Home

Let's be pleasant travelers because it's such a short ride.
—MONTE HALE

In 1991, tragedy struck closer to home. My son Mike, who was a diabetic, was visiting his brother Brad in Frazier Park, California, when he had a reaction to cotton candy he had eaten at a local fair. He passed out that evening at Brad's house. Before they could get him to the nearest hospital, which was sixty-five miles away, he suffered a massive heart attack and passed away. Sandy and I were devastated. Losing your friends, even friends as close and dear as Marty and Jimmy, is nothing like losing a child. It certainly makes you do some soul-searching.

It also got me to thinking about what I wanted to do with the rest of my life and where I wanted to do it. I wasn't sure about the former, but I was about the latter: I wanted to go back to Texas. The opportunity arose when I was contacted by an independent company about working in Dallas making music videos, and that sounded pretty good to both Sandy and me. We finally came home to Texas in January 1994 and took up residence in the Las Colinas area of Irving, a Dallas suburb.

Over the next couple of years, I made eighteen or twenty music videos, including one with Willie Nelson. Then I got hooked up with John Ashley, who had been an associate producer on *Apocalypse Now*, then later moved on to television with shows like *The A-Team*. At that time he was a producer on *Walker, Texas Ranger*, which filmed in Dallas, and he hired me as a line producer. They had only one episode left to shoot for the year, so my job wouldn't really start until the next season.

That last episode was to be a two-hour movie about a reunion of Texas Rangers. Ashley wanted me to play one of the Rangers, then he said, "The lead guest-starring role is perfect for Willie Nelson. Do you think you could get a script to him?"

"Sure I can." I did, and Willie agreed to do the part. He signed a contract based on nothing more than my say-so. "Have you read it?" he asked me.

"Yeah."

"It look okay to you?"

"Looks fine to me."

"Give me a pen."

I thought that was pretty nice. Then disaster nearly struck. The weekend before we were ready to start filming, Willie called.

"I'm supposed to go on tour with the Highwaymen next week." He had done an album called *The Highwaymen* with Waylon Jennings, Johnny Cash, and Kris Kristofferson, and it had been a huge hit, leading to the tour. "I'm not going to be able to do the show."

Well, that was a helluva note. Here we were ready to shoot, and our lead guest star was backing out on short notice. "What are we going to do?" Ashley asked me.

"How about Stuart Whitman?" I asked. "I think I could get him for you."

I had first met Stuart when he costarred with John Wayne in *The Comancheros*. He had done more than his share of television, guest starring in such shows as *Murder, She Wrote*, *Knot's Landing*, and *Fantasy Island*, and he had been one of the leads in *Cimarron Strip*. He had also received an Oscar nomination

Bob and Chuck Norris, on the set of *Walker, Texas Ranger* (1994).
Courtesy of Bob Hinkle.

for best actor in a leading role for playing a child molester in the 1961 movie *The Mark.*

Stuart agreed to do the role, and we overnighted a script to him. By the time he arrived in Dallas, he had his part memorized and ended up stealing the show. No offense to Willie, but I think Stuart was made for that role. I was also feeling pretty good about myself. Here I had barely started on *Walker,* and I had gotten Willie, lost Willie, and defused a crisis. Unfortunately, the one thing I couldn't do was save John Ashley's job. He was replaced the next season by Lenny Katzman, who brought in his own crew and cleaned house of Ashley's. I was unemployed again. But at least I was home in Texas, so I figured this was as good a time as any to retire.

Since I've been "retired," I've managed to stay busy. I worked for the Federal Emergency Management Agency (FEMA) for ten years. I make my rounds on the western film festival circuit, going to as many as six or eight a year with my singing cowboy friend Dale Berry of Dallas. It gives me a chance to reconnect with some of my old buddies and also to get out there among the fans who made my career possible—and the careers of the likes of Dub Taylor, Chill Wills, Dean Smith, and others.

One of my favorite stops is Alvin Davis's National Cowboy Symposium and Celebration in Lubbock, Texas, in September every year. Another annual event I enjoy is the James Dean Festival the last week of September in Jimmy's hometown of Fairmount, Indiana. I regularly attend and have served as grand marshal. Upward of thirty thousand people, from as far away as Australia, come annually to Fairmount to remember Jimmy and reflect on what might have been.

In 2006 I directed a pilot for Bandera Productions called *Who Shot Pat Garrett?* with my nephew Terry Tainter, who has a production company in Lynnwood, Washington. We shot it at Happy Shahan's ranch in Bracketville, Texas, where John Wayne's *The Alamo* was filmed. Bandera Productions is a group

Actor Dale Berry and Bob (2004). Courtesy of Bob Hinkle.

of investors from the Texas Hill Country town of Bandera, who put up the money for what was going to be an anthology, documentary-type series called *Stories of the Old West,* and we chose the Pat Garrett story for our pilot. I think we ended up with a pretty good half-hour pilot, if I do say so myself, but our target market was cable, and cable just wasn't interested in a half-hour show. That was the first thing I ever shot on HD and the first and only thing I ever made that didn't sell.

In July 2007 Evel Knievel called and asked me to come to Butte, Montana, to shoot a special for Monster Energy Drink, which was sponsoring a motorcycle jump as part of the Evel Knievel Days festival. My nephew Terry Tainter put a crew together, and we went off to Montana. The event drew about twenty thousand people, and some kid broke the world record. A twelve-year-old from Australia jumped over 195 feet, breaking Evel's record of 193. In November of that year, Evel passed away. He marked yet another in a long line of friends I've made in the entertainment business who have gone on. I'm starting to think I'm going to outlive them all.

As I look back over my life, I realize how lucky I've been to do the things I've done and meet the people I've met. It's almost a miracle that I ended up in the movie business in the first place. I had no education or training in the ways of Hollywood or even in theater. No high school or church plays, nothing to prepare me for a career both in front of and behind the camera. I made my way on guts and BS, heavily seasoned with luck—some bad but mostly good. I wouldn't trade my life for yours no matter what you offered me. I worked with the likes of Rock Hudson, Elizabeth Taylor, and Paul Newman. I made friends like Jimmy Dean, Marty Robbins, and Chill Wills. In 1947 I became an Eagle Scout, and in 1967 I became a 32nd Degree Mason. I acted, I directed, I wrote, I produced, and I fell down a lot.

And to top it all off, I married the queen of the rodeo.

I want to close with a poem from an unknown author that Monte Hale gave me while we were shooting *Giant*.

> Life is like a journey taken on a train,
> With a pair of travelers at each windowpane.
> I may sit beside you the whole journey through,
> Or I may sit elsewhere, never knowing you.
> But if fate should mark us to sit side by side,
> Let's be pleasant travelers because it's such a short ride.

Robert Hinkle Filmography

Motion pictures that Bob has been associated with are listed in alphabetical order by title. Each item includes the film's stars and Bob's role or position.

The All American, dir. Jesse Hibbs (Universal, 1953), starring Tony Curtis, Mamie Van Doren. Stunts.

All the Fine Young Cannibals, dir. Mike Anderson (MGM, 1960), starring Robert Wagner, Natalie Wood. Texas talk man.

The Badge of Marshall Brennan, dir. Al Gannaway (Republic, 1957), starring Jim Davis, Lee Van Cleef, Marty Robbins. Stunts.

The Bamboo Prison, dir. Lewis Seiler (Columbia, 1954), starring Robert Francis, Brian Keith. Extra and stunts.

Binion Big Country (1975). Produced and directed.

Broken Lance, dir. Edward Dmytryk (20th Century Fox, 1954), starring Spencer Tracy, Richard Widmark. Stunts.

The Broken Land, dir. John Bushelman (20th Century Fox, 1962), starring Kent Taylor, Jack Nicholson. "Dave."

Bronco Buster, dir. Budd Boetticher (Universal, 1952), starring John Lund, Scott Brady. "Colorado Bob."

Charge at Feather River, dir. Gordon Douglas (Columbia, 1953), starring Guy Madison, Frank Lovejoy. Stunts.

The Conqueror, dir. Dick Powell (RKO, 1956), starring John Wayne, Susan Hayward. "Monk" and doubled John Wayne.

Country Music (Universal, 1972), starring Marty Robbins, Sammy Jackson. Produced and directed.

Dakota Incident, dir. Lewis Foster (Republic, 1956), starring Linda Darnell, Dale Robertson. "Joe."

The Far Horizons, dir. Rudolph Maté (Paramount, 1955), starring Fred MacMurray, Charlton Heston. "Jake."

The First Texan, dir. Byron Haskin (Allied Artists, 1956), starring Joel McCrea, Jody McCrea. "Lt. Hargrove."

The First Traveling Saleslady, dir. Arthur Lubin (RKO, 1956), starring Ginger Rogers, Barry Nelson. "Pete."

Giant, dir. George Stevens (Warner Bros., 1956), starring Rock Hudson, Elizabeth Taylor, James Dean. Texas talk man.

Gun the Man Down, dir. Andrew McLaglen (Warner Bros., 1956), starring James Arness, Angie Dickinson. "Sheriff."

The Gunfight at Dodge City, dir. Joseph Newman (Allied Artists, 1959), starring Joel McCrea, Julie Adams. "Rafe."

Guns of a Stranger (Universal, 1973), starring Marty Robbins, Chill Wills. Produced and directed.

Hud, dir. Martin Ritt (Paramount, 1963), starring Paul Newman, Melvyn Douglas. "Frank."

I Killed Wild Bill Hickok, dir. Richard Talmadge (Allied Artists, 1956), starring Johnny Carpenter, Denver Pyle. Stunts.

King of the Khyber Rifles, dir. Henry King (20th Century Fox, 1953), starring Tyrone Power, Terry Moore. Stunts.

Kismet, dir. Vincente Minnelli (MGM, 1955), starring Howard Keel, Ann Blyth. Stunts.

The Long, Long Trailer, dir. Vincente Minnelli (MGM, 1953), starring Lucille Ball, Desi Arnaz. Extra.

Men of the Fighting Lady, dir. Andrew Marton (MGM, 1954), starring Van Johnson, Frank Lovejoy. Extra.

The Misfits, dir. John Huston (20th Century Fox, 1961), starring Clark Gable, Marilyn Monroe. Stunts.

No Place to Land, dir. Al Gannaway (Republic, 1958), starring John Ireland, Mari Blanchard. "Big Jim."

Oklahoma! dir. Fred Zinnemann (MGM, 1955), starring Gordon MacRae, Gloria Grahame. Stunts.

The Oklahoman, dir. Francis D. Lyon (UA, 1957), starring Joel McCrea, Barbara Hale. "Kenny."

Ole Rex (Universal, 1961), starring Billy Hughes, Bill Coontz. Directed and played "Sheriff McCarty."

The Opposite Sex, dir. David Miller (MGM, 1956), starring June Allyson, Joan Collins. Texas talk man.

Outlaw Treasure, dir. Oliver Drake (UA, 1955), starring Johnny Carpenter, Adele Jergens. "Frank James."

Riding Shotgun, dir. André De Toth (Warner Bros., 1954), starring Randolph Scott, Wayne Morris. Stunts; bucked off bronco.

River of No Return, dir. Otto Preminger (20th Century Fox, 1954), starring Robert Mitchum, Marilyn Monroe. Stunts; doubled Robert Mitchum.

The Robe, dir. Henry Koster (20th Century Fox, 1953), starring Richard Burton, Jean Simmons. Stunts; doubled Richard Burton.

Sign of the Pagan, dir. Douglas Sirk (MGM, 1954), starring Jeff Chandler, Jack Palance. Stunts.

Speed Crazy, dir. William Hole, Jr. (Allied Artists, 1959), starring Brett Halsey, Yvonne Fedderson. "Sheriff."

The Ten Commandments, dir. Cecil B. DeMille (Paramount, 1956), starring Charlton Heston, Yul Brynner. Stunts; doubled Charlton Heston.

Under Fire, dir. James B. Clark (20th Century Fox, 1957), starring Rex Reason, Harry Morgan. "Pvt. Finley."

White Christmas, dir. Michael Curtiz (Paramount, 1954), starring Danny Kaye, Bing Crosby. Extra.

White Feather, dir. Robert Webb (20th Century Fox, 1955), starring Robert Wagner, John Lund. Stunts.

Wings of the Hawk, dir. Budd Boetticher (Universal, 1953), starring Van Heflin, Julie Adams. Stunts.

Young Guns of Texas, dir. Maury Dexter (20th Century Fox, 1962), starring James Mitchum, Chill Wills. "Sheriff Simon."

TELEVISION

The television shows that Bob has been associated with are listed in alphabetical order by show title. Each item includes the contribution he made to the show or particular episode.

Annie Oakley: "Reno" in "Dude's Decision" (dir. George Archainbaud; 1957).

Bonanza: extra/stunts in various episodes (dir. N. McDonald; 1959).

Dragnet: "Big John" in "The Big Juke Box" (dir. Jack Webb; 1958).

Flight: produced "Test Pilot" episode (dir. Gerry Morton; 1959).

Frontier Circus: "Dave" in "Stopover in Paradise" (dir. Sydney Pollack; 1962).

Gunsmoke: rider in "The Mistake" (dir. Andrew McLaglen; 1956); cowboy in "Quint Asper Comes Home" (dir. Andrew McLaglen; 1962).

Hollywood Jamboree: produced and directed (1965).

The Immortal: filmed second unit for pilot (dir. Joseph Sargent; 1969).

The Life and Legend of Wyatt Earp: stunts in various episodes (dir. Frank McDonald; 1957).

Mission Impossible: filmed second unit for various episodes (dir. Joseph Sargent; 1970).

Sheriff of Cochise: "Bronco" in "Husband and Wife" (dir. Harve Foster; 1957).

Stoney Burke: filmed second unit for various rodeos (dir. Leslie Stevens; 1962).

Tales of Wells Fargo: "Mac" in "Deadwood" (dir. Boris Sagal; 1958).

Tombstone Territory: deputy sheriff in "The Assassin" (dir. Felix E. Fiest; 1957).

Wagon Train: stunts in various episodes (dir. Earl Bellamy; 1958).

Walker, Texas Ranger: third judge in "Deadly Reunion" (dir. Michael Preece; 1994).

You Asked for It: rode bucking barrel (dir. Robert Lees; 1954).

The Young Lawyers: filmed second unit, Boston, for pilot (dir. Joseph Sargent; 1970).

Acknowledgments

In my career I've flown planes, ridden bulls, done stunt work, acted, directed, produced, and taught folks how to talk like Texans. As I have looked back over the years while working on this memoir, it surprises me how full my life has been. I've met and worked with some of the most interesting and most famous people of the twentieth century, from singers and actors to presidents of studios and of countries. That's pretty heady stuff for an ol' rodeo cowboy from Texas. It makes me realize how truly blessed and lucky I have been.

While toying with the idea of writing a memoir, I happened to come across Hugh and Paula Aynesworth, two more in a long line of wonderful folks I've met in my life. When I told them I wanted to do this book, they put me in touch with Mike Farris, my writing partner, and I thank them for that. Mike and I hit it off right away and, over the months we've worked together, we have become fast friends. I had a head full of memories, but he was able to coax them out and put them down on paper in a way that made even my wife and kids think maybe I'd lived an interesting life.

Others who deserve wholehearted thanks include Mark Winslow at the James Dean Foundation, with whom I have been close over the years. My friend Jimmy brought us together. My thanks also to Warner Brothers Studio, which gave me my big break by letting me set up shop in Alan Ladd's old dressing room and work on *Giant*. The studio has continued to support me as I've pulled my life, particularly my experiences on *Giant*, together into words.

Thanks also to Alvin Davis at the Cowboy Symposium in Lubbock, Texas, who recommended this book to the University of Oklahoma Press. Special thanks, too, to Byron Price, Chuck Rankin, and the entire crew at the press who did such a wonderful job of producing this book.

My family has been very supportive of me in this endeavor. I'm sure I must have driven them crazy talking about the "good old days," but I couldn't have lived the full life I've had without them.

Last, I think of those whom I have met and lost over the years. This book is written in loving memory of James Dean, Rock Hudson, Paul Newman, Evel Knievel, Chill Wills, Marty Robbins, Natalie Wood, Monte Hale, Whitey Hughes and all my other friends who have gone on before me.

—Bob Hinkle

When Hugh and Paula Aynesworth first contacted me about this fascinating guy they had met who was looking for a writer to help tell his story, I was intrigued. Bob Hinkle sounded like a man who had an interesting story, but I figured I'd better talk with him first and see for myself. Once I did, I knew his was a story I wanted to help tell, if for no other reason than because I wanted to hear it myself.

Bob didn't disappoint. I found myself captivated by his tales of teaching Rock Hudson how to talk like a Texan, shooting rabbits and brawling in parking lots with James Dean, doubling for John Wayne in *The Conqueror*, visiting Elvis Presley at Graceland, and racing go-karts with Paul Newman. I can't count the number of hours we spent at our "office"—the

McDonald's in Forney, Texas—where I sometimes found myself so wrapped up in his stories that I almost forgot to take notes. For a baby boomer like me, it was tantamount to reliving my childhood and teen years, but doing so with someone who had actually rubbed shoulders and broken bread with the pop culture icons of the day. How could I not want to tell that story?

What started as a mere collaboration soon turned into a friendship. And so, for allowing me to be mentioned as a friend in a list that includes names like Marty Robbins, James Dean, Roger Miller, Chill Wills, Paul Newman, Natalie Wood, Lyndon Johnson, Elizabeth Taylor, and Evel Knievel, my deepest thanks to my friend Bob Hinkle. Also, my thanks to Hugh and Paula for making the experience possible.

The folks at the University of Oklahoma Press have been a dream to work with, starting with Chuck Rankin, who gave support, feedback, and advice at every turn, and Byron Price, who first saw promise in Bob's story. Thanks, also, to Cheryl Carnahan, whose copyediting made this a better book.

No matter how many times you read and reread a manuscript, some things still escape your notice. For helping me spot those things, I thank friends and family members who read and critiqued what I thought were finished pages but turned out not to be. They include Steve Davis, Cindy Grunwald, Andrew and Angela Jones, and Bill Morgan.

Last but most important, I thank my wife, Susan, who first taught me to turn on a computer many years ago. She has provided support, tolerance, a meticulous eye for editing, and anything else I needed throughout the process. This book exists in large part because of her.

—Mike Farris

Index

In this index, films on which Hinkle worked are followed by his role; for example, Giant *(film) (dialogue coach).*

Binion Big Country (short film)
(producer), 237
Biskind, Peter, 54
Blanchard, Mari, 152
Blatty, William Peter ("Bill"), 152
Blessing, Wag, 140
Blue Hawaii (film), 194n
"Blue laws," 105
"Bob's Tavern," 195
Boetticher, Budd, 25, 25n, 27–29
Bohlin Silver Saddles & Buckles,
240
Bonanza (TV), 141
Brady, Scott, 25
Breakfast at Tiffany's (film), 184
Briskin, Mort, 149
Brokaw, Norman, 157
Broken Lance (film) (stunts), 155n
Brolin, James, 239
Bromfield, John, 149
Bronco Buster (film) (stunts), 25–
26
Bronson, Charles (Charles
Buchinsky), 140
Brownfield, Tex.: Chill Wills visit
to, 151; and "the Flats," 161–
63; Hinkle big hit with R.J.,
161; Hinkle's hometown, 12–
14, 43, 62, 91, 144; and
Oldsmobile telethon, 149–51;
and *Ole Rex*, 176–77
Bryant, Bear, 124
Buchinsky, Charles (Charles
Bronson), 140
Bullitt (film), 125
Burton, Richard, 85, 139–40

Campbell, Glen, 209
Career, summary of, 251

Carpenter, Johnny, 154–56, 155n
Channing, Carol, 143
Cher, 61
Cheyenne (TV), 65
Cinema Pictures, Inc., 204–205
Ciudad Acuña, Mexico, 88–90
Claude, Tex. (near Amarillo),
183, 189–90
Collins, Joan, 142
Comancheros, The (film), 247
*Come Back to the Five and Dime,
Jimmy Dean, Jimmy Dean* (play),
61
Conqueror, The (film) (Monk),
142, 147
Cook, Bob, 238
Coontz, Bill (William Foster),
171, 171n, 205, 226, 231
Cosby, Bill, 203
Country Music (film) (produced
and directed), 229–31
Crawford, Joan, 36–37, 118
Crow, John David, 124
Crowe, Cameron, 230

Dakin, Bert, 29
Dakota Incident (film) (Joe), 142
Damone, Vic, 136
Daniels, Bill, 213
Daniels, Price, 213
Darnell, Linda, 142
Davis, Alvin, 249
Davis, Jim, 226
Dean, James ("Jimmy"):
competitiveness of, 72–76; and
contract negotiations, 116,
130–31; Cow Palace rumor
and, 115–16; death car bought
by, 114–15; death of, 126–27;

dinner at Barney's with
Hinkle, 46–48; driving
incident with Hinkle, 75–76;
funeral of, 134–35; guitar
incident and, 70–72; Hinkle's
admiration for, 44, 49;
Hinkle's coaching requested
by, 45–46, 180; and
homosexuality rumors, 136;
and improvisation at Hinkle's
suggestion, 97–98; and
jackrabbit hunting, 62–65, 76–
79; last scene filmed of,
120–21, 133–34; and "Little
Bastard" nickname, 92, 122; in
Marfa, Tex., 35; photo of, *128*;
playing "hooky" on *Giant*, 117–
19; *Rebel* director complains to
Hinkle, 52; rifle given to
Hinkle by, 80; rise and abrupt
death of, 42–43; Sandy's home
cooking for, 48–49, 113; as
scene stealer in *Giant*, 93; and
shooting incident, 76–79; song
by Eagles for, 45; "stalked" at
bullfight, 89–90; Stevens and,
94–95; western wear bought
by, 49–51; wrap gift to Hinkle,
121. See also *Giant*; Hinkle,
Robert; Taylor, Elizabeth
Dean, Winton (Dean's father),
48, 123, 136
Dean Smith: Hollywood Stuntman
(short film), 211
Del Rio, Tex., 88
DeNiro, Robert, 183n
De Toth, André, 139–40
DeWilde, Brandon, 185–87, 190,
197–99

DeYoung, Cliff, 189
Dialogue coaching by Hinkle.
See *All the Fine Young
Cannibals*; *Giant*; *Hud*; *Opposite
Sex, The*
Dicus, Bob, 204
Double post, 180
Douglas, Kirk, 176
Douglas, Melvyn, 184–85, 190,
197–98, 203
Dragonfly Squadron (film), 165
Dr. Heart (documentary), 205–
206
Drifter (Robbins album), 231

Eagles, The, 45
East of Eden (film), 4, 42, 44, 49,
119
Eastwood, Clint, 143, 145–46,
226
Easy Rider (film), 53
Easy Riders, Raging Bulls
(Biskind), 54
Eicke, Jack, 155n, 161
Elliott, Bill (Wild Bill Elliott), 29
Ellsworth, Bob, 140
Errair, Kenneth, 64
Evans, Clay, 75–76, 109
Evans, Vince, 240
Evans, Worth, 61, 75, 99
Evel Knievel Days festival, 250–51
Evelyn, Judith, 56
Exorcist, The (novel) (Blatty), 152

Fairmount, Ind., 47, 79, 121, 134,
249
Fair Park visit (Dallas, Tex.), 106–
108
Famous Artists Agency, 3